BRITAIN'S RAILWAYS
from the air

TEXT
JOHN GLOVER
PHOTOGRAPHY
IAN HAY

MYRIAD
LONDON

London Waterloo (right) is Britain's busiest station. The view here looks north across the station towards the Thames. The main train shed on the right was completed between 1899 and 1922, has a concourse 800ft (250m) long and includes a large stained-glass window over the main road entrance. The main Waterloo Bridge pedestrian entrance is surrounded by the Victory Arch, a memorial to company staff killed in both world wars. On the left is the long curving roof of the former Waterloo International Railway Station. From 1994 to 2007 this was the London Eurostar terminus for trains from London to Paris and Brussels. It closed when the high-speed rail link between London and the Channel opened in 2007 and St Pancras became its London terminus. Since then, the Waterloo International platforms have remained unused.

Previous page:
Bristol Temple Meads with the Brunel trainshed in the foreground.

First published in 2011 by Myriad Books Limited
35 Bishopsthorpe Road
London SE26 4PA

Photographs © Ian Hay
Text copyright © John Glover

ISBN   1 84746 382 7
EAN 978 1 84746 382 1

Designed by Jerry Goldie Graphic Design

Printed in China

www.myriadbooks.com

CONTENTS

INTRODUCTION

In 1830, the opening of the Liverpool & Manchester Railway ushered in a new era of transport, for goods and for people. No longer was the galloping horse the fastest that man could travel; George Stephenson's *Rocket* achieved *thirty miles per hour!* The railways provided the ability to move goods cheaply and in large quantities, just what an expanding industrial economy needed. Sustained periods of rapid growth saw a huge railway network peak at around 32,000 miles of route (51,000km) in 1930; it is about half of that today. Railways shaped Britain, but Britain also shaped the railways. To what extent was the line of route dictated by engineering requirements? How were water barriers of rivers and estuaries to be tackled? Should you go over the hills or tunnel through them? Would the penetration of historic towns and other sites prove impractical? How would the railway professionals react to these challenges? This book introduces a new perspective to such questions by examining the British railway system through the medium of modern aerial photography. It must be conceded though that buildings seen from above are not necessarily as elegant as they may appear from ground level.

Stations, and major stations in particular, feature throughout this book. Their architecture varies from the mundane to the spectacular. Many have been altered, extended, or completely rebuilt over the years, and change will continue. Of particular note is the way in which stations relate to the towns and cities they serve, and how they (and the lines that serve them) have influenced urban development in general. They also need to be accessible. A station right on the edge of town or in a greenfield site is going to have a rather different clientele than one sitting squarely in the middle of the shopping and business districts. Stations in suburban or rural areas are a different story again.

Railways have also brought about great engineering achievements, notably bridges and viaducts, some of which are illustrated. There are also the supporting features, such as yards and depots needed for the railway businesses. The railway has evolved organisationally. Briefly, around 120 private railway companies were compulsorily amalgamated into the "Big Four" in 1923, which were nationalised as British Railways in 1948. Following the 1993 Railways Act the network was then privatised. This book follows a geographical layout based on railway lines and routes, starting with Kent, moving clockwise round Britain and finishing in London.

The aim of this book has been to produce a comprehensive cross-sectional view of Britain's railways from above in the context of their surroundings. It may perhaps cast some new light on their contribution to the Britain we know.

John Glover

Right: Harringay West station (just in view) where the author was once a booking clerk, with Hornsey station in the distance.

SOUTHERN

The Southern railway companies encompassed everything south of the Thames and extended west as far as Padstow. But unlike those serving the industrial North, there was little in the way of freight traffic generators to supply the company with core traffic. And so the Southern turned to the passenger market and built what became the greatest suburban electrification system in the world under the guidance of Sir Herbert Walker. That encouraged and developed housebuilding and great volumes of London commuter traffic. Other important businesses were traffic via the Channel ports, the carriage of the armed forces, especially the army and the navy, race traffic (Epsom and Ascot for example) and holidaymakers to the South Coast resorts.

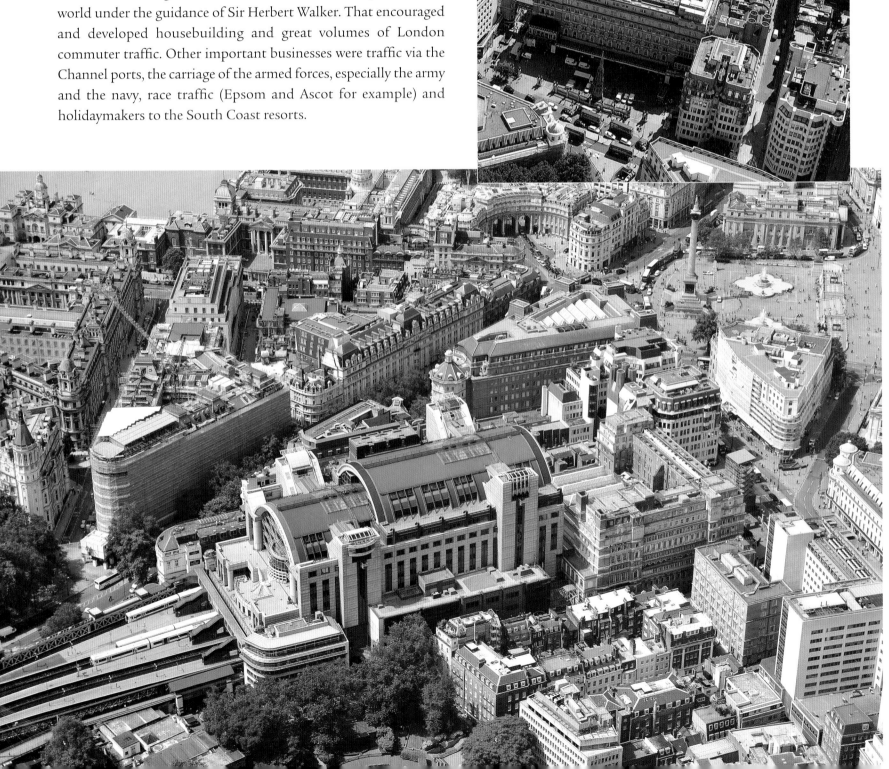

London Charing Cross *left*

This busy West End station has only six platforms. It was opened in 1864. Like its Cannon Street neighbour with which the South Eastern Railway served the City, it is the work of engineer Sir John Hawkshaw and architect Sir Charles Barry. Built on the site of Hungerford Market, the view over the railway bridge which carries the Hungerford name can be seen (top), and also the hotel on the station frontage with the Eleanor Cross in the forecourt. The platform area (bottom) has been covered in with a 1990s office block, Embankment Place. The station is close to Trafalgar Square, and Nelson's column can be seen. This is, to all intents and purposes, the centre of London.

London Cannon Street *above*

Cannon Street suffered heavily from bombing during the Second World War and the station roof was later removed entirely. Like Charing Cross, Cannon Street is very close to the Thames, and little more is left of the original building than the platforms (now seven) and the pair of red brick towers each 120ft (37m) high. Vacant air space in a well-placed location in the City has been much sought after, though subsequent building over the tracks has left the station with a very basic and functional feel. Like most City establishments, use at weekends and on Sundays in particular is very limited and the station's timetable reflects the fact that commuter traffic is greatly reduced at these times.

Borough Market *above*

After leaving Waterloo East, the four lines from Charing Cross are joined by those from Blackfriars, and then converge into two in the top right of this picture. They then meet the lines from Cannon Street at the former Borough Market Junction (bottom left) before entering London Bridge Station. There is also a single track chord (right) to allow trains to run between Cannon Street and London Bridge. This photograph shows a train from the London Bridge direction heading towards Charing Cross. Underneath all this can be seen Borough Market itself. The road to the left is Borough High Street.

Southwark *left*

Southwark Cathedral takes pride of place in this view from the Borough Market area, but looking towards London Bridge Station. The positioning of the cathedral shows the considerable diversion that the railway had to make to get round it, though the cathedral did well from selling the relatively small portions of land for railway building. The result was a severe curve in the track, which has been a challenge to the operators ever since.

London Bridge

This is the "country" end of London Bridge Station, with the Thames and various City landmarks in the background. As can be seen, there are really two separate stations; that in the foreground is the Brighton company's terminus, the other (at a slightly higher level) is for the South Eastern routes to Charing Cross and Cannon Street. There are 17 parallel tracks at this point, one of which on the through lines has no platform. They are connected by subway, but the large numbers of passengers changing between platforms use the very substantial bridge seen here. Railways can and do shift a great number of people but their use of land as seen here is often not quite as economical as it could be.

Chislehurst *left*

For many people Chislehurst, in the London Borough of Bromley, epitomises leafy suburbia. This is the view of the four-platformed station from the south-easterly direction, with a train approaching on the down slow line from Charing Cross.

Slade Green *below*

Trains need depots in which to stable, but most importantly places where they can be serviced and maintained. Depots are also a base for train crew. This is Slade Green, a little to the west of Dartford, which caters for the local services on the North Kent lines and others. As can be seen, depots can be quite space-consuming. In the middle of the trains in the foreground there are two running lines which carry the ordinary train services. Clearly, based on the number of trains in the depot, the photograph was not taken during peak hours; it was, in fact, taken at 09.20 on Sunday 20 June 2010.

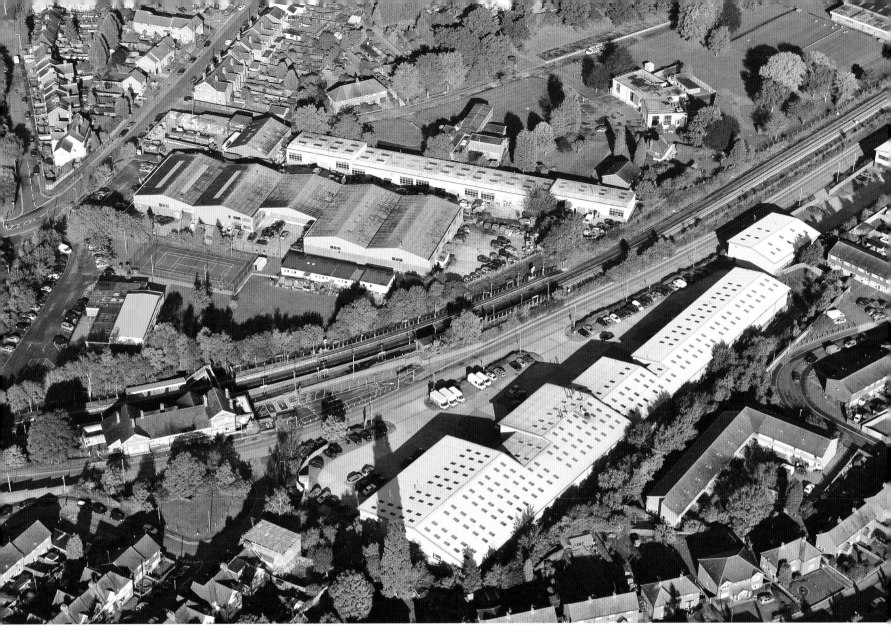

Bat & Ball *above*

Bat & Ball station is a mile to the north of the centre of Sevenoaks and was opened in 1862. It was named after a public house, long since gone, although the station is in Bat & Ball Road. The *Beer in the Evening* guide reassures us that there are still 302 pubs within 10 miles (16km). The 1881 census records that the Station Master was Mr Edward Gratrick aged 32 from Camberwell, who lived in the station house with his 23-year-old wife Sarah from Ramsgate, and their eight-month old daughter Ann, born in Swanley. They also had a domestic servant, Alice Wiffen from Croydon, aged only 14. Also recorded at that address is William Ranger, aged 24, a railway fireman and presumably a lodger. Today the building is boarded up and the station is unstaffed.

Eynsford *right*

The evening sun catches the country station of Eynsford at the edge of this Kent village. There are up and down platforms, 1862 station buildings, an ageing wooden shelter with decorative canopy and a concrete footbridge. The bus has just left and is about to turn into the A225 which will take it, behind the railway, to Sevenoaks.

Ebbsfleet International *above* Folkestone *right & below*

This view is of the large Ebbsfleet International station; domestic services call at the central platforms, while the others are for international trains. The line leaving the high-speed platform is the connection to the North Kent lines (Gravesend, Chatham etc), which has its own platforms. While the journey time from St Pancras is only 17 minutes the housing development planned close to the station has yet to be built. The large car parks indicate that future passenger numbers are expected to be high.

The sheer size of the Channel Tunnel complex at Folkestone is brought out well in this view from above the M2 motorway, which passes to the south of the site. Next to it are the arrival lines for the Eurotunnel Shuttle services, which sweep round in a tunnel to reappear at the terminal to the rear. Here there are 10 separate tracks, for passenger and goods shuttles respectively. Access is via the sloping approaches reached from the four overhead routes. The two on the left are for loading, the others for unloading. A close-up of one of these may be seen bottom left. Through the middle of it all sweeps a Eurostar international passenger service. These trains are 430 yards (394m) or nearly a quarter of a mile long.

Maidstone East *left*

This station, which was originally run by the now-defunct Chatham company, offers a direct journey to London. This service was considerably faster than that of its dilatory neighbour the South Eastern, which winds its way up the pleasant Medway Valley from Paddock Wood to Maidstone West, continuing on to Strood. The three-platformed Maidstone East station is distinguished by the long ramped slopes between the street and the platform, which were in place years before the needs of those with disabilities received any attention. To the right can be seen the bridge crossing the Medway, and the main road is the A229 motorway feeder. The Royal Mail sorting office is distinguished by the fleet of red vans. This view is taken looking south-east; the railway towards Ashford (left) immediately enters a succession of two short tunnels.

Darenth Viaduct *below*

This viaduct in Kent passes over the river of that name. The view is towards the north-west, showing a London-bound train approaching Farningham Road station, just out of the picture. The Darenth flows north, and after passing through Dartford reaches the Thames in about four miles. By then it forms the boundary between Kent and Greater London.

Ashford International

This longitudinal view of Ashford International from the east shows High Speed 1 (HS1), the Channel Tunnel Rail Link, cutting through the centre of the picture. Raising the high speed connection above ground level on Ashford viaduct enables the pre-existing railway connection to the Canterbury West line (right) to be maintained. However, trains on HS1 can also call at Ashford through loops laid in the track. Which platform is used depends on whether the train is a Eurostar, for which customs and immigration formalities are required, or a domestic operation. There are also three electrification systems: HS1 is ac (alternating current) overhead only, the local railway dc (direct current) third rail, and the domestic HS1 trains are both. The tracks, bottom, lead to Dover, and those off to the left are the non-electrified branch to Hastings. The lower picture shows the international station building, left, and the bridging leading to the centre international platforms, numbers 3 and 4. The remainder are for domestic traffic and are connected to each other by subway. This can be entered from either side of the station. The "spare" bridge to the car park is there only for emergency exit purposes.

Elephant & Castle

"The Elephant", as it is commonly known, is usually thought of as a huge gyratory. But it is also the southern terminus of the Bakerloo Line and a station on the Northern Line of London Underground. Not very obviously from street level, but well illuminated from above, is the four-platform railway station situated on a viaduct. This night view is from the north looking towards Herne Hill. In the centre of the picture is the Strata building, also known as "The Razor", on account of the three wind turbines on its roof. Completed in 2010, it has 43 storeys and contains a total of 408 flats. At 480ft (147m) high, it is the tallest residential building in London.

London Blackfriars

Blackfriars was the City terminus of the Chatham railway company, but importantly it is also where the Thameslink route crosses the river to link rail services north and south. Major works to complete this project are seen underway in these two pictures taken in spring 2010. The platforms are being extended with the result that there will be station entrances sited on both the north and south banks. This also requires the re-siting of the tracks to avoid conflicts between what will in effect be two separate sets of services. As can be seen, rail and road bridges run in parallel, while the stumps of the long since dismantled second rail bridge lie in between.

BRIGHTON LINES

London Victoria

London Victoria was built as two separate stations in 1860-62, and the join still shows. Originally, there was no direct public access between the two parts. The main photograph looking towards the buffer stops shows the Chatham side (services to Kent) on the right, with the station roofs undergoing reglazing, while the Brighton side (south London and beyond to the South Coast) left, is mostly covered over above platforms 9-18. Fortunately, the glass roof above the concourse was retained, which makes that part of the station light and airy. The second picture shows the same scene from the direction of the station frontage. Beyond that, trains leaving Victoria have a stiff pull up the curving Grosvenor Bank, before reaching Grosvenor Bridge across the Thames with its nine tracks. After this the routes from each section of the station diverge to Brighton, straight on, or to Kent, left.

The Grosvenor carriage sheds are to the left of this picture, emphasising the size of building which is needed to keep vehicles under cover. The road bridge on the right is Chelsea Bridge.

Selhurst depot *above*

Selhurst depot, north of Croydon, lies in between the lines to Victoria (near side) and London Bridge (far side). By constructing it here, the company provided easy access to and from both sets of lines, which was a definite advantage. On the other hand, there are still curvature problems, and nothing ever faces in the right direction!

Crystal Palace *left*

The station now known as Crystal Palace was once Crystal Palace Low Level, but this distinction was made unnecessary with the closure of High Level (on a separate site) in 1954. This reflects a chequered history; when the Crystal Palace burnt down in 1936, it needed a considerable effort to recover the railway traffic lost. The Low Level station is a diverging junction and consists of two parts. The grander (centre) offers services towards Sydenham. These include London Overground for which the platforms have been increased from the two shown here to four, and the more modest part (semi-obscured) which accommodates trains to West Croydon and Beckenham Junction. The whole forms a remarkable complex of buildings with stairways everywhere.

East Croydon *below*

East Croydon is one of those stations where growing traffic volumes are putting ever more pressure on its ability to cope. The Brighton was never a company which built more facilities than it needed, and using East Croydon's triple island platforms and modest station entrance as constructively as possible is quite a challenge. Unusually, the links from the concourse to the platforms and the subways connecting the platforms are all slopes. This can give rise to high-speed collisions between those anxious to catch trains and those toiling up them to reach the station exit. This view looks east; the tracks on the road outside the station and stretching into the distance are those of London Tramlink, which also provides a direct route to West Croydon station.

Oxted

This station is well situated in the centre of the Surrey town of Oxted, although the railway does tend to separate the town into two halves. The main station buildings are on the up (west) side and are joined to the down side by the ubiquitous Brighton company subway. A bay platform on the down side is sometimes used to run a connecting shuttle to Uckfield, when this branch is not provided with a through service from London Bridge. This view looks north-east. To the south, Oxted viaduct takes the line over the A25 and the river Eden in a wooded setting; this is undulating land and the railway soon enters Limpsfield tunnel. It emerges at Hurst Green, where the electrified line to East Grinstead diverges from the diesel-worked line to Uckfield.

Reigate *above*

Reigate station is on the east-west route from Tonbridge to Guildford and Reading; in this view looking towards Reading an electric train from London has arrived. It will go no further, as this is the limit of the third rail. The main services here are provided by diesel trains which serve Gatwick Airport. The level crossing at the platform ends is at the bottom of Reigate Hill and can result in long tailbacks. This road descends from the North Downs ridge, to the right.

Purley *left*

This is where the branches to Caterham and Tattenham Corner leave the Brighton main line (bottom centre) and then diverge from each other almost immediately. This accounts for the six platforms which have from time to time been used for dividing/joining trains from the two branches. However, the present service pattern is half-hourly Victoria to Caterham, half-hourly London Bridge to Caterham, and half-hourly London Bridge to Tattenham Corner. A 12-car train is arriving at platform 1 on the up fast line, en route for East Croydon, in a view taken from the south-east. The sidings beyond the station deal with gravel traffic, and the road beneath is the A22.

23

Brighton

Brighton station faces due north and the area has a complex of very constrained railways. These are (main picture) the line which curves sharply to the west on the coastal route to Hove and beyond, that heading for London, and that just visible curving to the east for Lewes. The large number of houses in the foreground may be noted, together with the height at which they are situated above platform level. The further two pictures show what that means in practice, in terms of the height of the wall separating them from the station. There are eight platforms. The front of the station is also shown.

Lewes *above*

This is often thought of as the station which most retains the essence of a traditional country junction, in this case serving the county town of East Sussex. Light and airy inside, there are views of the South Downs from the platforms. Looking towards the station entrance on the road bridge, the lines from Victoria are seen on the left, and from Brighton on the right. Trains for Eastbourne and Seaford proceed straight ahead. A long footbridge within the building provides access to all platforms. One of the central platforms has no rail track – it was removed following the closure of the line from Uckfield in 1969. Future restoration of the track to its original purpose would not be difficult.

Eastbourne *below*

The station at Eastbourne is a terminus, and a well appointed one at that. The clocktower in the street outside stands out well, announcing the station's presence. This view from the west shows just how long 12-car platforms can be at about 800ft (290m) and how far passengers often have to walk to reach the front of the train. It also demonstrates that a station such as this can manage with just three platforms. Train operation at Eastbourne is made more complex by the need for trains from London to Hastings to reverse here, although the station also provides an opportunity to reduce train length over the final section of the route.

Littlehampton *left & right*

These two photographs of Littlehampton show the
heart of the station (left) and the view looking north-
west from above the railway (right). Littlehampton
station has a straightforward layout with four platforms
and there are two in use here. To the left of the
platforms is the meandering river Arun, which allowed
Littlehampton to develop as a minor port. Beyond the
carriage sheds, the line can be seen as far as the junction.
Here the left-hand route carries trains to Ford and
the right-hand route – just visible in the photograph
– to Horsham or Brighton.

Ford *below*

Ford is a modest West Sussex village on agricultural
land close to the river Arun. Most of the population
live south of the 1846-built station, seen here with a
Southern train travelling west. Despite its rural setting,
Ford has a remarkably good service with 10 trains per
hour: three to Bognor Regis, one to Portsmouth &
Southsea, one to Southampton Central, two to London
Victoria via Horsham, one to Brighton and two to Littlehampton. This is because the station is a passenger
interchange, sited conveniently at the hub of these lines.

London Waterloo

Waterloo's 24 platforms are clearly visible in this photograph. The station has more platforms than any other station in Britain, and that total does not include the Waterloo Underground or the four platforms at Waterloo East. The five Eurostar platforms (seen here in the long curving shed) have been disused since the company transferred to St Pancras. Waterloo remains an impressive station, which largely assumed its present form when major rebuilding was completed in 1924. This view along the Thames takes in Westminster Bridge, the London Eye outside County Hall, Hungerford Bridge carrying the railway and a footbridge on each side from Charing Cross, and Waterloo Bridge. The lines leaving the station have to curve before taking up their direction of travel. This will not make it easy to extend the low number platforms 1-4 on the inside of the curve, so they can take longer trains as is planned within the next few years.

To the rear of the concourse are the rail offices (right). There is a covered pedestrian link from the main Waterloo Station to Waterloo East which keeps passengers separated from road traffic.

Vauxhall *above*

The station at Vauxhall is wholly situated on a viaduct. It provides a useful link to the Victoria Line of London Underground and to the bus station immediately outside. The area is known as Vauxhall Cross and the end of Vauxhall Bridge itself is visible to the right. The large building with a green finish is that of MI6, the Secret Intelligence Services. A nearby road is named Bondway, but the name seems to be more to do with the storage of bonded goods than any link with a master spy.

Clapham Junction *left & above*

Clapham Junction is a junction, but perhaps only half-heartedly so. For passenger services it is more a series of broadly parallel tracks with a total of 16 platforms. Each is allocated to a specific destination and that is a great help to newcomers in finding their way around. Thus Bournemouth trains leave from platform 9, Brighton trains from platform 13, and so on. It is a system that isn't quite foolproof, but is not far off. In the main view from the London end of the station and from left to right there are three groups of four lines. These are for the Brighton company (to East Croydon), then the South Western (to Woking

and branches). These are followed by extensive carriage sidings, and then a final four for the Reading/Windsor lines, again for the South Western. At both outer edges there are platforms which are used for trains to and from the West London line to Kensington Olympia. All platforms are joined by a very long and wide footbridge, which can take rather longer to negotiate than the congested subway located where the tracks come together. But at least there is space to run on the footbridge if you are late for a train! In the smaller photograph, the installation of new lifts can be seen.

31

Richmond *above*

This photograph shows Richmond station from the south. The two nearest platforms (1 and 2) are used by South West Trains for the Reading and Windsor service and platform number three is a bay which provides a connection to the District and North London Lines which use platforms 4-7. The North London Line is now operated by London Overground, with services to Stratford in east London. The station is a Southern Railway reconstruction and fronts on to the busy and congested Kew Road. Perhaps it is ironic that the road junction with the A316 in the background is named Richmond Circus.

Wimbledon *left*

This view looks from Wimbledon station towards London with the main station entrance and forecourt left. From left to right the platforms are used by London Underground (4), South West Trains (4), Thameslink (1) and London Tramlink (1). This is an example of a well-connected station which benefits from being on good through routes as well as being a natural terminus for tram and Underground lines. Retail development in the 1980s saw a second entrance/exit opened at the other end of the footbridge within the station.

Dorking *left*

An 8-car Class 455 unit of South West Trains stands in Dorking, once known as Dorking North. The station is a good walk from the centre of the town but there are bus services outside. In the background is the A24 road and the bridge over it to the left is that carrying the Tonbridge-Guildford-Reading line with Dorking Deepdene station on the near side. The station contains all the essential elements but it was not designed as conveniently as it might have been.

Guildford *below*

This station has eight platforms, two of which (platforms 6 and 7) have only one track between them as can be seen in the photograph. This allows passengers to board and alight from both sides provided the doors are released by the train crew. The footbridge in the foreground acts as a useful secondary station entrance; the main exit (and the town centre) are diametrically opposite.

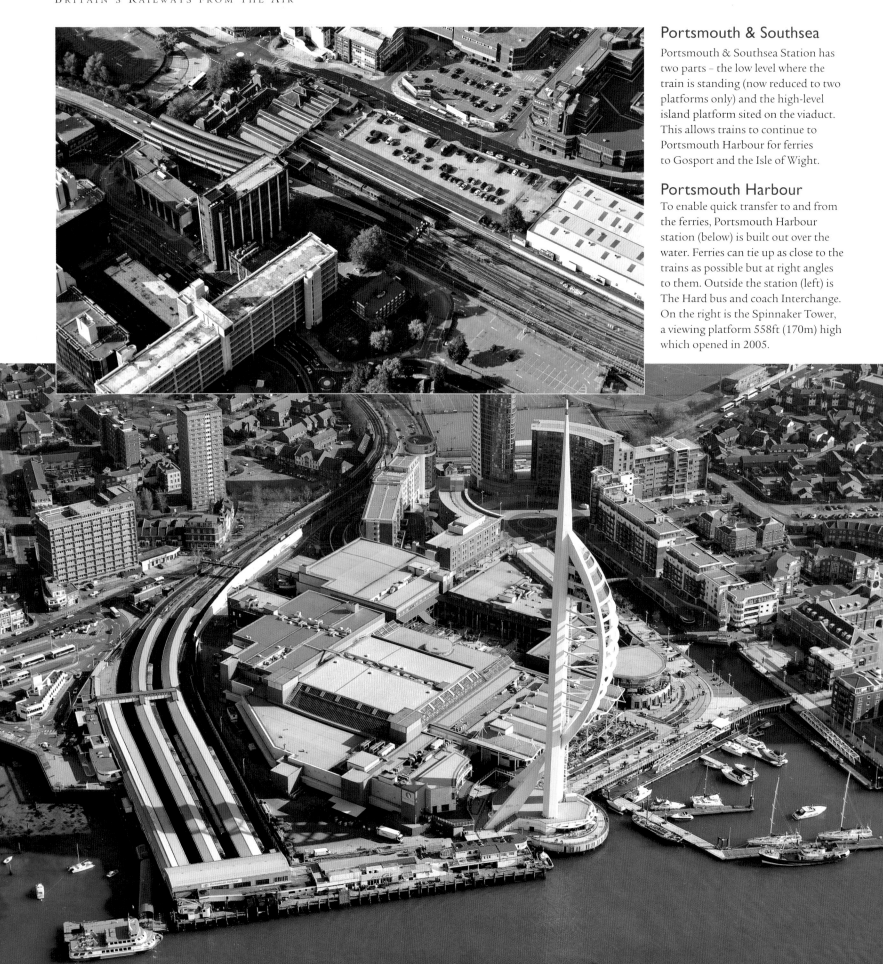

Portsmouth & Southsea

Portsmouth & Southsea Station has two parts – the low level where the train is standing (now reduced to two platforms only) and the high-level island platform sited on the viaduct. This allows trains to continue to Portsmouth Harbour for ferries to Gosport and the Isle of Wight.

Portsmouth Harbour

To enable quick transfer to and from the ferries, Portsmouth Harbour station (below) is built out over the water. Ferries can tie up as close to the trains as possible but at right angles to them. Outside the station (left) is The Hard bus and coach Interchange. On the right is the Spinnaker Tower, a viewing platform 558ft (170m) high which opened in 2005.

Southampton Central

The main photograph shows Southampton Central Station from the south-west. The station consists of a central island platform and two side platforms connected by a wide footbridge and steps. Passenger access is available from both sides. Southampton may be a city but in the days of British Rail it achieved InterCity status for journeys to Birmingham but not to London. On the south side, the buses are seen taking passengers directly to the ferries. The name Southampton Central is a bit of a misnomer; travelling east, the railway soon runs into a tunnel, and the centre of the city is above the tunnel.

Bournemouth depot *above*

This depot was built for the original Bournemouth electrification of 1967 and is sited on the track bed of the Somerset & Dorset Railway on the approach to its Bournemouth West terminus. Incoming trains (from the left) reach the inspection and maintenance shed (in the foreground) before continuing to the carriage washer and toilet flushing apron. They then reverse to the carriage cleaning shed or one of the storage sidings. The seemingly back-to-front nature of the depot is due to its entrance being by reversal from the down side platform in Branksome station, with outward movements being the opposite of this.

Weymouth *left*

What was once a large sprawling station at Weymouth has been reduced to just three platforms. From the buffer stops, it is a short walk to the town centre or the beach. The now moribund Harbour Branch leaves the main line some distance before reaching the terminus.

River Tavy viaduct *above*

The Tamar Valley line from Plymouth to Gunnislake begins by following the Devon bank of the Tamar then crosses the river on a bridge at Calstock. Before reaching Bere Ferrers station, the line has to cross the mouth of the Tavy where that river flows into the Tamar. The resultant eight tie-arch viaduct seen here is 1,490ft (454m) long. With stonework approaches, the bridge is supported on cross-braced tubular iron pillars.

Okehampton *left*

The station at Okehampton lay on the former Southern route from Exeter to Plymouth but passenger services were withdrawn in 1972. Part of that line remained open for freight traffic from Meldon Quarry and the route to the former Coleford Junction is now owned and operated by Aggregate Industries. From 1997, there have been limited passenger services from Exeter for the benefit of walkers and Dartmoor Railway has also run limited services to Meldon. All passenger operations centre on Okehampton station, which has been substantially restored.

WESTERN

The Great Western Railway was built to link the cities of London and Bristol; en route the railway engineering town of Swindon was created to serve the line. The railway soon expanded, with the company's single Paddington terminus in London serving most of the West Country, South Wales, part of the West Midlands and through to Birkenhead. The line also carried substantial freight traffic especially coal from the Welsh valleys. Today Great Western runs a comprehensive express passenger service using an ageing fleet of High Speed Trains plus an extensive network of secondary and local services. Only the line to Heathrow is electrified. The proposed east-west Crossrail link through Central London is presently under construction and when completed will carry many existing Great Western services.

London Paddington

Paddington station dates from 1838 but in 1854 was moved to its present site to accommodate growing traffic. This resulted in a curve rather than a straight line into the station. The main photograph looks out over the station neck and the prominent Bishop's Bridge Road which crosses the site. Construction of both the main station and the Underground station was a joint venture between the Metropolitan Railway and the Great Western. The main rail lines are on the left and London Underground's Hammersmith & City lines on the right. Beyond that is West Westbourne Bridge, then Ranelagh Bridge which is followed by the Underground's Royal Oak station. Then comes Lord Hill's bridge, after which Underground services cross to the other side of the formation. The last road bridge carries the Great Western Road on which the Hammersmith & City Westbourne Park station entrance is sited. That railway turns left here and immediately afterwards the A40(M) Westway crosses the main formation. There are several views of the north side of the station and Paddington Basin, which is linked to Little Venice and the Grand Union Canal. At the front of the station is the Great Western Hotel.

Maidenhead *above*

Maidenhead Station is on the original line of the Great Western Railway which opened as far as Reading in 1840. It is the junction for Bourne End and Marlow, hence the track bearing off to the left. In this view from the west, the curious shelter on the branch platform can be seen. One train is waiting here; the train for London has recently departed but is still in sight, and the Reading train is on the down platform. Maidenhead's connections will improve significantly in future years as it is the planned western terminus of Crossrail.

Taplow *right*

The Great Western Railway was designed by the leading civil engineer Isambard Kingdom Brunel (1806-1859). The Great Western's use of "Broad Gauge" railway track (7ft 0 $\frac{1}{4}$ in / 2,140mm) resulted in the track spacings being rather wider than on most of the British system, and the more open look can be seen here at Taplow. Rolling stock too can be a little wider than standard, but this makes its use less flexible.

Reading *above*

Reading is a major junction and an important commuter
link to London and the west. Rail passenger services
approach Reading from London Paddington, London
Waterloo, Basingstoke, Newbury and Bristol/Oxford via
Didcot. There are also freight services including containers
from Southampton and to the Midlands and North.
This view looks north-west over the station complex with
a Waterloo train just visible bottom right. Future plans
are to increase station capacity by the addition of more
platforms and also to remove conflicting train paths
wherever possible through the use of tunnels or elevated
junctions. The down main line in particular will then be
free of many potential hold-ups. South Western trains to
Reading are electrified on the direct current (dc) third rail
system but it is planned to electrify all main line routes
through Reading in the next few years.

Henley-on-Thames *right*

This is the neat terminus at the end of the single track
branch from Twyford to Henley-on-Thames. Other stations
on the London side of Reading are those to Greenford,
Windsor & Eton Central and Marlow.

WEST OF ENGLAND

Newbury *above*

The Berks & Hants line is the direct route from London to Taunton and the West of England and also to Newbury, one of the principal towns in the section west of Reading. This photograph looks towards London and shows four tracks through the station with the platforms on loops off the main line. The centre of Newbury is a short distance west of the racecourse which has its own station. Future plans are to electrify the line at least to here.

Westbury *right*

This station is about a mile (1.5km) from the town of Westbury in Wiltshire. It is a railhead for freight traffic, notably aggregates, and also a major passenger junction serving the Reading to Plymouth Line, the Wessex Main Line, the Heart of Wessex Line and local services to Swindon. In this view from the north-west, the station is in the distance and the lines from it diverge towards Taunton (right) and Salisbury. Approaching is the Westbury Avoiding Line, which will pass under the route to Salisbury and then make its own junction with the line to Taunton.

Exeter St David's

The principal station in this city is that of the Great Western, where the railway runs north-south. It is situated in the valley of the river Exe which, as these photographs show, runs alongside the railway before passing underneath it through a bridge on the line to Plymouth. The steeply curved line rising to the right is that of the South-Western to Exeter Central, half a mile (1km) away. The capacious six-platform station of St David's has five through lines and one bay; between this and the river can be seen the diesel unit depot. In addition to the main line services to London Waterloo and those from London Paddington to Paignton and Penzance, local trains operate on the ex-South-Western lines from Exmouth through to Barnstaple.

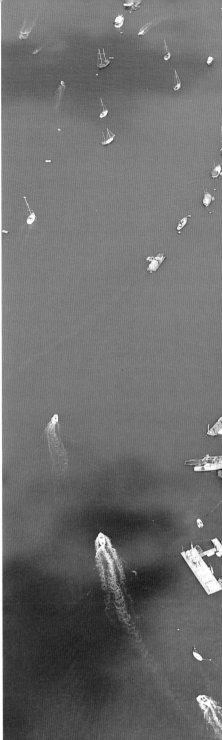

Dawlish Warren *left*

The route from Exeter to Plymouth runs along the western shore of the river Exe as it broadens out into an estuary, before turning to the west along the exposed coastal stretch at the bottom of the cliffs. This view is of Dawlish Warren and its station. Just to the north, a passenger ferry operates between April and October from the Starcross Pier in the distance across the mouth of the Exe estuary to Exmouth.

Kingswear

British Railways relinquished the 6.5 mile (10.5km) Paignton to Kingswear branch in 1972. The line was an extension of the branch from Newton Abbott which BR retained. The railway is now run as a heritage line by the Dart Valley Railway who carry mainly summer holiday visitors to Kingswear, where a ferry takes passengers across the river Dart to Dartmouth. These views show how the railway, hugging the edge of the Dart, reaches its terminus at Kingswear by passing over a small bridge. Formerly railway operated, the ferry premises on the far side (which are now a restaurant) have the distinct appearance of a station without any track.

Plymouth *left*

Laira is a major traction maintenance depot situated in Plymouth. From east to west the depot consists of 10 stabling sidings, a smaller building where underframe cleaning takes place, the High Speed Train (HST) maintenance building and the workshops. A through freight route to Plymouth Friary still passes round the depot.

Saltash *below*

Brunel's crowning glory was the opening of the Royal Albert Bridge at Saltash (below) in 1859 shortly before his death. This bridge has two main spans each 455ft (139m) long with the rails 100ft (30.5m) above high water level. The Tamar road bridge alongside was completed in 1961, bringing to an end the long existing Saltash foot and car ferry. This view was taken from the north-east looking towards Cornwall.

St Austell *right*

The construction of the railway through the undulating Cornish landscape, with its deep river valleys, meant that viaducts were common-place. Originally built from timber for reaons of economy, all have now been replaced by masonry arches. St Austell Viaduct is one of two substantial viaducts west of St Austell station. Viewed here from the north-west, this viaduct is 621ft (189m) long.

St Ives *above*

Heading south-west, the last branch of the railway on the Cornish peninsula is from St Erth to St Ives. At St Ives, the traveller is 303 ³/₄ miles (489km) from London Paddington. Originally the line went as far as the end of the curve (of the old platform) seen on the right of the photograph. But as also happened elsewhere, this branch was shortened by 396ft (120m) in 1971 when the land was sold for use as a car park.

Didcot

It is at this important junction that the line splits: one branch heads north to Oxford and one towards Wootton Bassett Junction in the west, where the lines to Bristol and South Wales part. In the foreground is Foxhall Junction, at the western end of the Didcot complex; the station is out of the picture to the right. Trains approaching from the west can continue to Oxford (left), or towards the station and Reading (right). There is also a separate direct line between the station and Oxford. Thus trains for Oxford approaching from Bristol or South Wales can only call at the six-platform Didcot Parkway by reversal; this is of course irrelevant for freight. The result is a triangle of lines and it is always difficult to make constructive use of them. The main use here is as a car park, and there is a footbridge at the far end (out of sight) which gives access to the down station platform. The car park is also used as a market on Sundays. At the top and beyond the freight yard can be seen the premises of the Great Western Society, a 1930s engine shed, now a museum housing a unique collection of Great Western Locomotives, rolling stock and railway artefacts. In this and the inset photograph can be picked out the traverser which moves rolling stock sideways, Didcot Halt together with the level crossing, the signal box and water tank, and a short length of broad gauge track.

Swindon

Swindon's grand Victorian railway station was demolished in 1972 and replaced by a modern station with a single island platform, with signals in each direction and a bay for the Gloucester services at the eastern end. However, this was found to be too restrictive and a platform on the down main line was reinstated (main picture). This view looks towards Wootton Bassett; the Great Western Railway's former rail works are on the right-hand side of the line. Swindon was chosen as the location for the GWR's engineering workshops. These extensive premises were finally closed in 1986 and the land has largely been redeveloped. It does however house the STEAM museum run by Swindon Borough Council, which tells the story of the works and the history of the GWR. Much of the area to the front of the works (bottom left) has now been cleared but on the other side of the line (bottom right) can be seen the rows of houses which the GWR built for its workforce in the 1840s. The Railway Village, as it was called, consisted of 300 cottages for railway workers and their families. Brunel designed the first row of cottages and supervised their construction.

Bristol *above*

The original Bristol Temple Meads (seen at the top but no longer with any track) was completed in 1840 by Brunel as a western terminus to the GWR. The station was expanded when it also became a terminus for the Bristol & Exeter Railway completed in 1844. In later years, the Bristol and Gloucester Railway, the Bristol Harbour Railway and the South Wales Union Railway joined them. To accommodate the ever-increasing number of trains, the station was rebuilt in the 1870s and again in the 1930s. The result was the large 13-platform station seen here from the south. Notable is the turreted station entrance designed in the 1870s by architect Francis Fox which presides over a long and ornate forecourt leading down to the main road.

Bath Spa *right*

The railway at Bath Spa had to be accommodated next to the river Avon and the double crossing of the river which can be seen in this view was neatly executed. Visible here are St James Viaduct (left) and Dolemeads Viaduct (right). Bath expected a station in keeping with the city's elegant architecture and the Tudor-style station designed by Brunel delivered this. The entrance to the station, which is Grade II listed, faces the city, on the opposite side of this photograph.

Weston-super-Mare *above*

This substantial seaside resort is the nearest to the West Midlands and, since the arrival of the railway in 1841, Weston has enjoyed an influx of visitors. The station, the third main station to be built in the town, was constructed in 1884 and is on a single track loop which leaves the Bristol & Exeter main line at Uphill Junction. Photographed to the north of this, the three-platform Weston-super-Mare station can be seen to the left of the point where the prominent A370 crosses the railway.

Severn Tunnel *right*

The first Severn Bridge was built in 1966, bringing to an end the ferry service and an earlier car carrier service run by the railway between the two sides of the Severn. Wide estuary crossings like the Severn have always been a problem for rail bridge-builders and the Great Western Railway opened the Severn Tunnel at the early date of 1886 – a great feat of engineering for the time. The tunnel is 4 miles 628 yards (7km) long although only 2¼ miles (3.62km) are under the river. The railway at the bottom right corner is that from South Wales to Gloucester, which eventually curves away from the M4 and out of the picture to the left. On its left, again at the bottom, a row of trees separates it from the railway in the cutting. At the end of this is the mouth of the Severn Tunnel. On the upper left the complex of buildings on the Welsh side is Sudbrook Pumping Station, which prevents the tunnel from being flooded.

Newport *left*

A major reconstruction of Newport station in South Wales has been in progress over the last few years. The new station has four platforms with two through tracks. Platforms 3 & 4 on the north-west side (left in the photograph) are for the fast lines; the others and platforms 1 & 2 are for the relief lines. The previous station had a single entrance on platform 1, which meant a long walk for passengers coming from the north-west side most of whom had to cross the station footbridge. The new arrangement gives access from both sides of the railway and the round buildings on either side have full ticket offices. Beyond the end of the platforms and the river Usk viaduct, the line to Hereford leaves the route to the Severn Tunnel Junction. All the lines go through the Newport tunnel in the foreground.

Cardiff

The main station serving the capital city of Wales is Cardiff Central but there is also the well situated Cardiff Queen Street on the route up to the Valleys, and Cardiff Bay on the one-mile single track branch to the former docks area. West of Cardiff Central is Canton maintenance depot and the junction for the line to Barry. The main picture (top) shows Cardiff Central station from the north-east and the Taff River Viaduct close by with the city bus station just outside. The station has only eight platforms with two through lines. Those on the far side (platforms 7 & 8) are for the Valley lines; when they leave to the west they rise and cross the main line, as shown in the photograph (right). This photograph also shows the entire length of the branch to Cardiff Bay. The docks are beyond and the stretch of water to the left is Atlantic Wharf. The view of the large depot with Cardiff Central station in the background (left) shows its comprehensive facilities. The line to Barry leads off to the right. This photograph also features the city's famous Millennium Stadium.

Pontypridd *left*

From this Valleys town there is a choice of two rail routes: the Merthyr Line (right) which runs from Cardiff, Merthyr Tydfil and Aberdare and follows the Taff Valley or the Rhondda Line (left) which goes from Cardiff to Treherbert. The Rhondda Line follows the Methyr Line as far as Pontypridd and then continues along the Rhondda Valley. The diesel unit in this photograph has left the station and is crossing the Merthyr viaduct. It is bound for Merthyr Tydfil or perhaps Aberdare.

Treforest *below*

Just south of Pontypridd is Treforest where the river Rhondda flows into the river Taff. The station here is a no-frills two platform affair with a footbridge and a ticket office. Treforest has a very regular six trains per hour service, all of which start at or come through Cardiff Central.

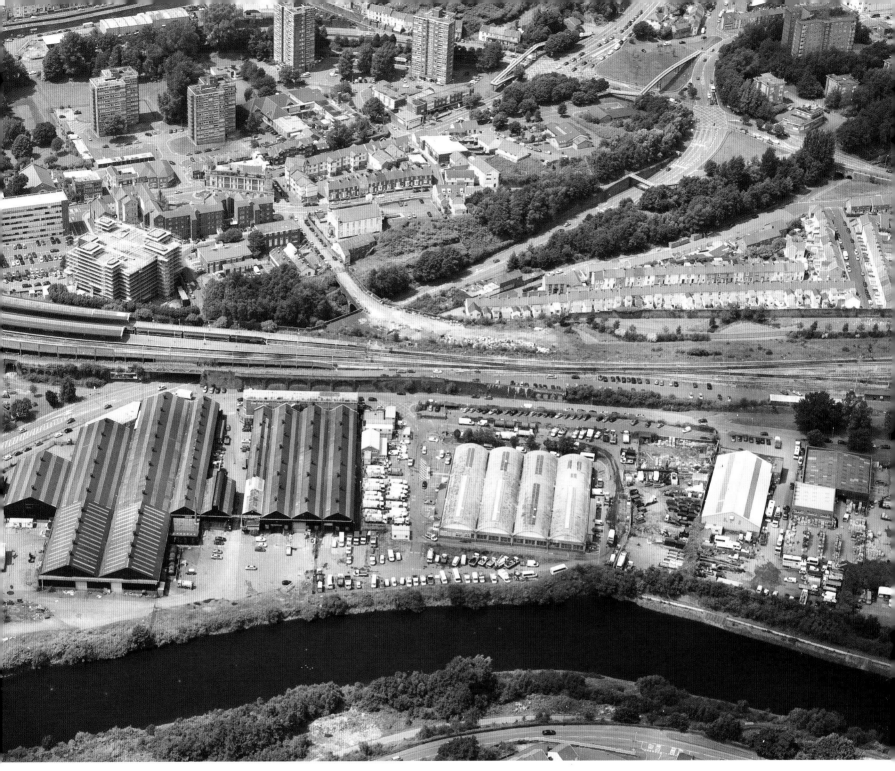

Brecon Mountain Railway *left*

The Brecon Mountain Railway runs from Pant, shown here, for three miles to Pontsticill and Dol-y-Gaer alongside the Taf Fechan Reservoir. This is narrow gauge locomotive no 1, *Graf Schwerin-Löwitz*, built in Germany in 1908. It entered traffic in Wales in 1981, and has since covered 125,000 miles (200,000 km), equivalent to more than 20,000 round trips. Most of the route is on the trackbed of the old Brecon & Merthyr Railway, which opened in 1854 and closed in 1964.

Swansea *above*

In the late 19th century Swansea and its environs were served by seven stations. The sole survivor, Abertawe/Swansea, is the western terminus for trains from Cardiff which means that trains to and from east Wales have to add a couple of miles to their journey when visiting the town and reverse out of the station if they are proceeding further. Destinations to the west include Pembroke Dock, Carmarthen, Milford Haven and Fishguard. The river Tawe is in the foreground.

THE JOINT RAILWAYS

While the route between London and Bristol was that of the Great Western and that to Crewe was part of the London & North Western (LNW), the area in between was less defined. Much of the Great Western route to Birkenhead was later closed, and the company came to joint working agreements elsewhere with both the LNW and the Great Central. Centres such as Shrewsbury had several incursions, while the main route between Birmingham and Bristol was part of the Midland Railway. Changing fortunes of successor companies over the years have seen this broad segment of the railway undergo many changes, and there is no reason to believe that these are at an end.

GREAT CENTRAL

London Marylebone *left*

The last main line into London, until the advent of High Speed 1 from the Channel Tunnel, was the Great Central Railway to Marylebone in 1899. It is doubtful if the London extension of this railway was ever very profitable and during the 1960s much of the line closed and Marylebone station became something of a backwater. At one stage the conversion of the London end of the line into a route for buses was being seriously considered. As the main photograph shows, Marylebone has a grand station frontage. This was designed by Henry William Braddock, a civil engineer for the Great Central Railway. Services are operated to Aylesbury and to Birmingham, with some extended to Kidderminster. Oxford will be reached via a new connection. Since Chiltern Railways took over the station in 1996, Marylebone has undergone a complete facelift and two extra platforms have been added making six in all. Passenger numbers have grown massively in the last 10 years and Marylebone is now London's fastest growing rail terminal in terms of passenger numbers.

Rickmansworth *above*

A relative latecomer, the Great Central Railway became dependent on the established operators for various joint agreements, notably with the Metropolitan and the Great Western. Rickmansworth station was opened by the Metropolitan in 1887 with the Great Central added in 1899. A Marylebone to Aylesbury train is seen in this photograph. The main station building on the near side has a porched entrance resting on pillars. This is placed in a long low single-storey brick building with four chimneys – a reminder that stations such as these were dependent on coal heating for many decades of the 20th century. A subway joins the two platforms, which each have substantial canopies. Railway electrification stalled here from 1925 to 1961, during which time Rickmansworth was a changeover point between electric and steam traction for Underground services. That led to much activity, with the running of steam and electric locomotives through the station, the provision of a holding siding at each end, and water supplies for the steam locomotives.

Bicester North *above*

Today Bicester North services are provided by Chiltern between London Marylebone and Birmingham Snow Hill. Bicester North station was once reduced to a passing loop in 27 miles of single track but double-line running has now been restored throughout from Princes Risborough to Banbury. The recent two-level car park was installed as a means of creating much needed new car parking capacity.

Aylesbury *left*

The layout of Aylesbury station has recently been improved and simplified, with the previously unused bay platform on the west side now part of the car park. The station was once the responsibility of three companies through two joint Boards, the Metropolitan (Met/GC) and the Great Western (GW/GC). The companies did not always agree on strategy and were often reluctant to invest in areas away from the centre of their operations. All services are now operated by Chiltern. A new station has been opened at Aylesbury Vale Parkway serving areas to the north of the town. The diesel unit servicing depot (right) is north of the station.

Banbury

This is an important station on the CrossCountry route, where services continue to Birmingham and beyond. There are also direct services to London. The station was reconstructed between 1956-58 under the 1955 British Railways Modernisation Plan and apart from the number of platforms being reduced from six to four, the layout has survived largely intact from that time. The station even retains old-fashioned semaphore signals which use a pivoted arm to signal to train drivers. The general view of the station from the west side (lower picture) shows the main entrance; it is not possible to reach any platform without using the bridge. The diesel unit in the bay platform (no 4) is either on the move, or it is keeping as far away from the passengers as possible! The view from the east shows a Freightliner train heading south.

Worcester

From London, Worcester can be reached either via Oxford or Birmingham. The main photograph shows Worcester Shrub Hill Station from the east side. To the right are the lines to Droitwich Spa and Birmingham and curving away to the left is the line to Great Malvern and Hereford. A diesel unit can be partly seen on the chord (line) which enables Droitwich to be reached without reversing at Shrub Hill. Beyond that junction is the bridge over the Worcester & Birmingham canal and the town centre with Foregate Street Station is in the far distance. Foregate Street has a very convenient city centre location although Shrub Hill is a more suitable location from the point of view of the railway network. Also shown is a closer view of Shrub Hill, which still uses semaphore signals.

Shrewsbury

This dramatic station was designed in 1848 by the architect Thomas Penson in an imitation Tudor-style to match the buildings of Shrewsbury School (now Shrewsbury Library) opposite. The station acts as a "gateway to Wales" and serves a large number of destinations as can be seen in the photographs. The upper view looks towards the town centre, while the lower shows the station forecourt and entrance. These are guarded in a perhaps abstract way nowadays by Shrewsbury Castle, a regimental museum. The footbridge over the railway gives quick access to HM Prison which is immediately in front of it on the far side. The lines to the left lead to Wrexham and Crewe respectively, those on the right across the river Severn to Wolverhampton, to Craven Arms for Hereford and Llanelli, and to Aberystwyth. The river follows a complete ox-bow round the City centre, and reappears on the left. The two principal road bridges across it are named English Bridge and Welsh Bridge respectively, reminding people of how close Shrewsbury (*Amwythig*) stands to the Welsh border. The station operator is Arriva Trains Wales.

Wrexham General

Originally, there were two stations on this site sitting side by side. Wrexham General was operated by Great Western and Wrexham Exchange by the Great Central Railway. Both were through stations and both in commercial competition with each other. Now, only one station – Wrexham General – remains and there are even physical connections between the two original sets of lines. In this photograph which looks north, the former Great Western line to Chester (platforms 1 & 2 on the right) links with the Great Central route to Bidston and New Brighton on the left (platform 4). They are connected via the line on platform 3. The steps to the bridge indicate the difference in levels between the two sites. The Great Central single track (below) continues to a terminus less than half a mile (0.7km) away at Wrexham Central which sits in the heart of the town.

WEST COAST MAIN LINE

Stretching north from London Euston to Glasgow Central, with offshoots to Birmingham, Manchester, Liverpool and North Wales, the West Coast Main Line is the backbone of Britain's railway system. Most of the line was electrified between 1960 and 1975. It is very busy and has recently been modernised. Nevertheless, buoyant traffic growth will see it again reaching its maximum capacity, for which the building of a new High Speed Line (HS2) is seen as the answer. Also included in this section is the Midland Line from London St Pancras to Carlisle, in some ways a competitor but in reality serving the East rather than the West Midlands, and then following the magnificent route over the Pennines to Carlisle.

London Euston

Established as the London terminus of the London & Birmingham Railway in 1837, Euston was a grand station built on a grand scale. But piecemeal development over the years led to the controversial decision to demolish the station and its original entrance, the Euston Arch. The present building dates from the mid-1960s. The front of the station is dominated by four black office towers, behind which the low station buildings appear very modest. A large concourse is followed by ramps to the 18 platforms all covered by a largely solid roof rather than the glazed trainshed roofs of the original. Part of the area above the concourse was used as a parcels depot but this has now long been abandoned. Beyond that, the lines can be seen leaving the terminus, en route for Camden and the Primrose Hill tunnels. In front of the entrance is a bus station, and the Euston Road. On the right-hand side of the station (to the east) is Eversholt Street and Euston House, once the headquarters of the British Railways Board. The railway end of Euston station shows how comprehensively most trains are hidden within the station complex; the buildings in the foreground are the Ampthill Estate.

Wembley Central *right*

When sporting events and concerts are taking place at nearby Wembley Stadium, Wembley Central has to deal with large crowds but the main line platforms normally have only an hourly service. As can be seen, most of this station has been built over as a commercial development and the general effect is rather depressing. In this view looking north, a local train is on its way to London Euston; these two tracks on the west side of the main line are shared with London Underground Bakerloo Line services. The tracks have a different electrification system of dc (direct current) fourth rail, compared with the ac (alternating current) overhead of the rest. Crossing above the train is the Chiltern Line, which has its own Wembley Stadium station out of the photograph to the right.

Ledburn *left, below & above*

The Great Train Robbery was a notorious episode of railway history. In the early hours of 8 August 1963, an overnight postal train on the West Coast Main Line was travelling from Glasgow to Euston. Fifteen masked robbers cut the lineside signal and telephone wires, blocked the green signal with an old glove and lit up the red signal using a six-volt battery. When the train came to a halt, they overpowered the train crew and the postal staff. They then uncoupled the locomotive and the first two coaches carrying the valuable

registered mail and forced the driver to continue another mile to an underbridge. Here, 120 mailbags were thrown down to a waiting lorry. The bridge near which the train was first brought to a standstill is seen above with a Virgin Pendolino passing beneath it, and also in the distance in the north-facing view on the left; at the time of the robbery this was a level crossing. The second bridge where the actual robbery took place can be seen in the foreground and also in the inset picture. The robbers' haul was valued at £2,631,784, mostly in used banknotes and which they later used to play games of Monopoly when holed up in a rented farmhouse. At that time, the maximum compensation for a lost registered packet was £20.

Cheddington *right*
This is the view looking towards London at this quiet location on the West Coast Main Line one mile south of the robbery site. The village of Cheddington is another kilometre beyond the station. You can still see the curve where the branch line from here to Aylesbury had its platform, and beyond it the route taken by the line over what is now a road. The branch closed in 1953; its impression on the landscape remains over half a century later.

Castlethorpe *above*

The scene above of two trains passing each other is a fine sight; captured in the Castlethorpe area, the trains are a Virgin Pendolino and a London Midland Desiro. The former is on the down fast line, the latter on the up slow; their closing speed will be at least 200mph (320kph).

Leighton Buzzard *left & right*

A station at Leighton Buzzard was first opened in 1838. The present station is a British Rail reconstruction; its importance can be gauged by the large footbridge and extensive car park. Those who wish to exit to the far (west) side of the line do have to negotiate a second bridge. Immediately north of the station are the Linslade tunnels, 861ft (262m) long; both ends are visible in the second photograph. These are made up of a single tunnel on either side and one double-track tunnel in the centre. Initially, train drivers were said to be apprehensive about approaching what appears to be a very small tunnel entrance in a tilting train travelling at 125mph. Beyond the tunnels to the top right is the Grand Union Canal. This runs broadly parallel to the railway for many miles and then its route deviates away from the railway.

Milton Keynes Central

In the decades after the Second World War
a number of "new towns" were constructed.
Milton Keynes was one of the last to be
designated in 1967. The main photograph
shows clearly the grid pattern of roads on
which Milton Keynes is laid out with the railway at the bottom. The new station was opened
in 1982 and in recent years the number of
platforms has been increased to seven. Also in
the Council's area are the stations of Wolverton,
Bletchley, Fenny Stratford, Bow Brickhill and
Woburn Sands. Milton Keynes Central is a
principal stop on services from Birmingham
New Street to London Euston and from Crewe
to London Euston. There are also services on
the Marston Vale Line and to Bletchley and
Bedford. Since 2009, Milton Keynes Central
has benefited from an hourly service to
East Croydon.

Coventry

Coventry station lies just south of the city's inner ring road. The first station in the city was built in 1838; in 1840 it was moved to its current location a short distance to the east. The station is largely a legacy of the rebuilding of the entire city centre in the 1960s and follows the general approach of several others on the West Coast Main Line with grey concrete and glass and angular architecture. The city centre is on the left-hand side of this photograph. The main line sweeps through the area in a gentle curve. In the foreground is the junction where the line towards Nuneaton diverges from that to Birmingham; at the other end of the station there is a similar junction where the line towards Leamington Spa leaves the main line – seen here just in front of the train approaching from London Euston. Only the main line is electrified here and that provides three fast services and one stopping train each hour between Birmingham and the capital.

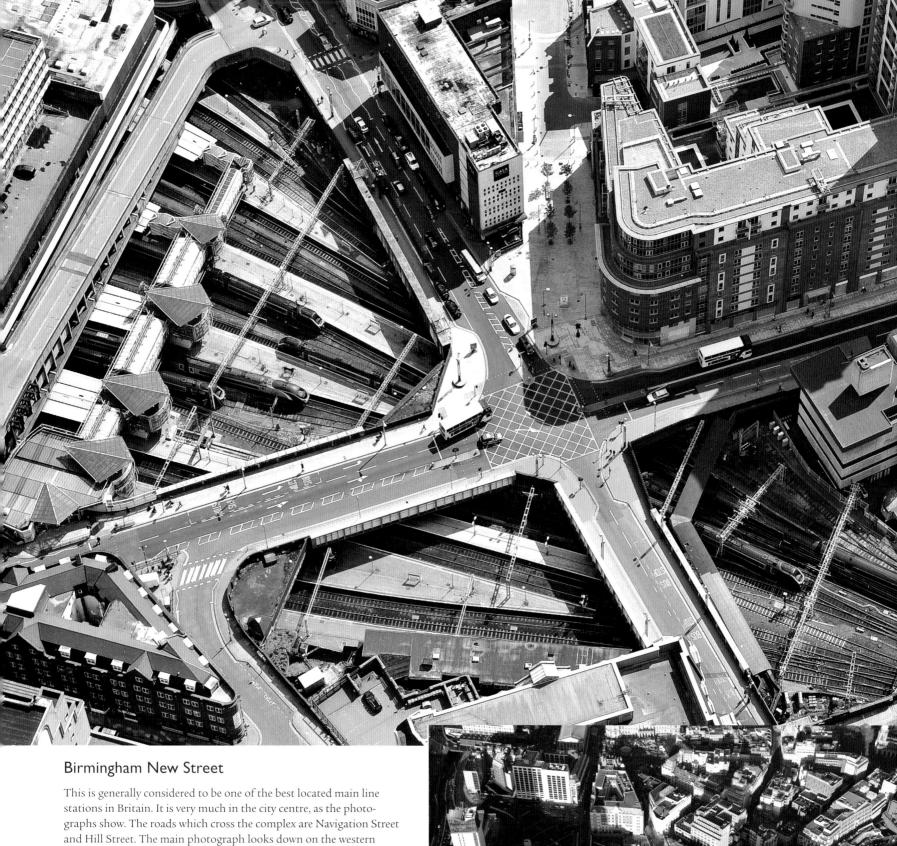

Birmingham New Street

This is generally considered to be one of the best located main line stations in Britain. It is very much in the city centre, as the photographs show. The roads which cross the complex are Navigation Street and Hill Street. The main photograph looks down on the western end of the station with trains to Bristol above and to Wolverhampton below. Both rail routes enter tunnels immediately after leaving the platforms. The 1960s listed signalbox can also be seen, as well as some of the 12 platforms that make up the station. The more general view shows how the station fits together, with the station buildings (and shopping arcades) covering the centre of the station area. Further junctions may be found at the other end of the station where trains to Lichfield, Derby and London diverge.

Lawley Street *right*

Beyond the eastern end of Birmingham New Street and slightly to the north lies the container terminal of Lawley Street (centre). The electrified line to the left is that to Lichfield and the first station of Duddeston is visible. To the right are the lines to Derby and in the distance the (freight) line between Aston and Stechford crosses the picture. The West Coast Main Line to London is just out of sight to the bottom.

Selly Oak *above*

Situated approximately two miles (4km) south-west of Birmingham city centre, this station is on the Midland Railway line to King's Norton which eventually leads to Bristol. The simple station design has a couple of canopies plus a footbridge, a ticket office and little else. At the top of the photograph is the A38 road, and to the left, in the line of trees, is the Worcester & Birmingham canal. Local electric services run between Lichfield Trent Valley (Staffordshire) and Redditch (Worcestershire), outside the Centro (West Midlands) area at both ends.

Wolverhampton

This station is on the site of the former High Level station built by the London & North Western company in 1852. The station has been extended in recent years principally by the addition of the new platform seen on the right of the photograph. Passengers use the new bridge to access the platforms. The bay that is mainly used for the non-electrified Shrewsbury service is well hidden from passengers unfamiliar with the station. The bottom photograph also shows the site of the former Great Western (Low Level) station buildings constructed in 1855, now bereft of railway facilities. This station closed in 1972, and the track bed from Birmingham, other than the last section into Wolverhampton, is now used by the Midland Metro.

Crewe

Crewe Station was erected in 1837 when Crewe had barely 100 residents. The Grand Junction Railway established a rail engineering works in the town two years later and built 200 cottages for its workers. Crewe soon developed as one of the most important railway centres in Britain linking the four largest cities in England and making the station one of the most famous in the world. Crewe was the first station to have its own railway hotel (the Crewe Arms, built in 1838 and still in existence) and it was the first to form a junction between the rail systems of two private companies. The photograph shows the station from the north-west and demonstrates the extent to which the platforms have been reduced because there are now fewer stopping services at the station. Nevertheless Crewe retains 12 passenger platforms. South of Crewe (left) are the Basford Hall sidings. They are flanked (left) by the two down independent lines. These tunnel under the lines to Chester and then surface (for Liverpool) or remain in the tunnel under the main line and surface to join the route to Manchester. The up lines start with those electrified on the right-hand side. The view of the carriage sheds shows the West Coast Main Line in the foreground and behind the recently electrified line to Kidsgrove.

NORTH WALES COAST

Conwy *left*

The magnificent Conwy Castle is situated on a rocky outcrop on the west bank of the river Conwy. It was built by Edward I as part of a chain of castles designed to establish English rule in Wales. The original road bridge seen here is now a footbridge and was built by Thomas Telford in 1826. Next to it is the railway bridge built by Robert Stephenson in 1848. Its wrought-iron tubular construction is similar to that used by Stephenson to construct the Britannia Bridge across the Menai Strait further along the line. Both Telford and Stephenson designed their road and rail bridges in a castellated style to blend with the castle. The A347 is now carried on the bridge to the left.

Colwyn Bay *below*

With Prestatyn, Rhyl and Llandudno, Colwyn Bay is one of a series of popular seaside resorts which stretch along the North Wales coast. All the resort stations have long platforms; those at Colwyn Bay can accommodate 12 coaches. Today the stations have a slightly down-at-heel appearance, their heyday perhaps in the past as more visitors use the A55 Expressway. The road runs along the front behind the railway here; elsewhere it is between the railway and the beach.

Menai Bridge *above*

Road and rail links to Ireland, particularly to Dublin, were of vital military and political importance to Britain. The A5 road and the rail route which carried goods and passengers to Holyhead (and then by ship to Dun Laoghaire or Dublin) were established when Ireland was governed from Westminster. The railway crossing of the Menai Straits to Anglesey was a tricky engineering problem since the bridge needed to be high enough to allow ships to pass underneath but strong enough to carry the considerable weight of a train. The magnificent Britannia Bridge, designed by Robert Stephenson and opened in 1850, is 1,380ft (421m) long. The bridge was strengthened by the use of wrought-iron tubes but these were largely destroyed by fire in 1970. The Britannia Bridge was then rebuilt as a joint road/rail bridge. It can be seen in this view which looks east along the Straits towards Telford's earlier road bridge, erected one mile (1.6km) to the east. The town of Menai Bridge is on the left, Bangor on the right.

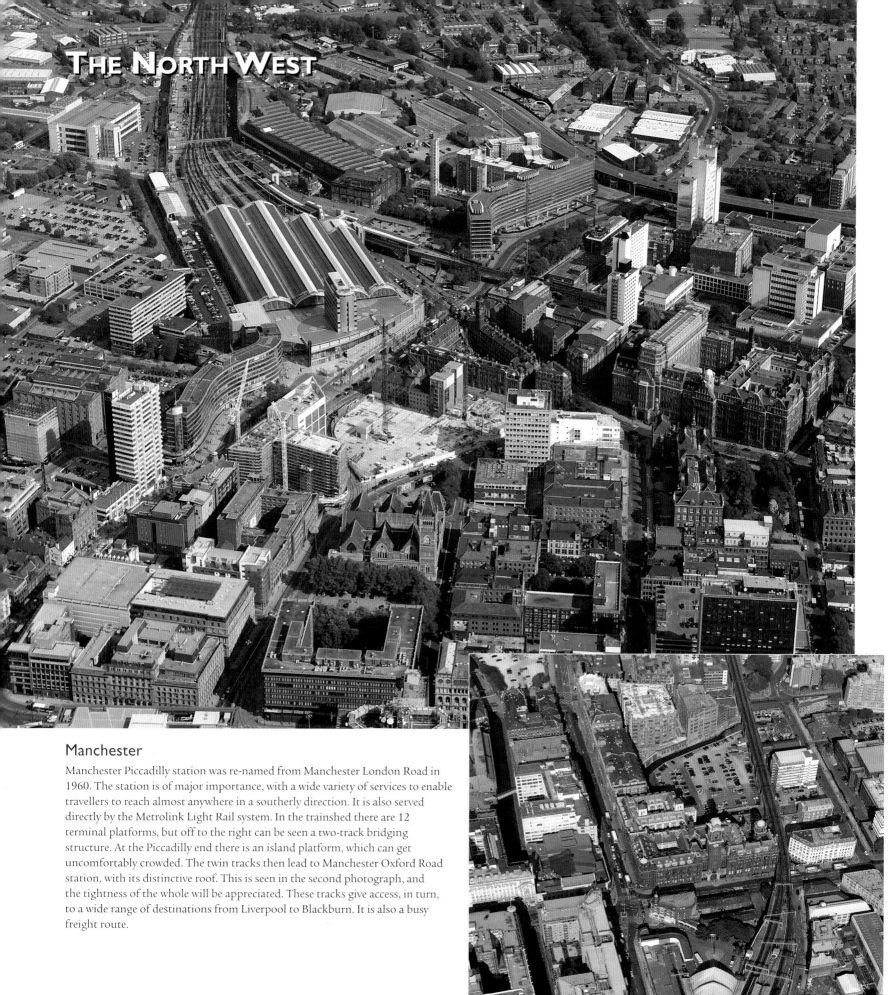

THE NORTH WEST

Manchester

Manchester Piccadilly station was re-named from Manchester London Road in 1960. The station is of major importance, with a wide variety of services to enable travellers to reach almost anywhere in a southerly direction. It is also served directly by the Metrolink Light Rail system. In the trainshed there are 12 terminal platforms, but off to the right can be seen a two-track bridging structure. At the Piccadilly end there is an island platform, which can get uncomfortably crowded. The twin tracks then lead to Manchester Oxford Road station, with its distinctive roof. This is seen in the second photograph, and the tightness of the whole will be appreciated. These tracks give access, in turn, to a wide range of destinations from Liverpool to Blackburn. It is also a busy freight route.

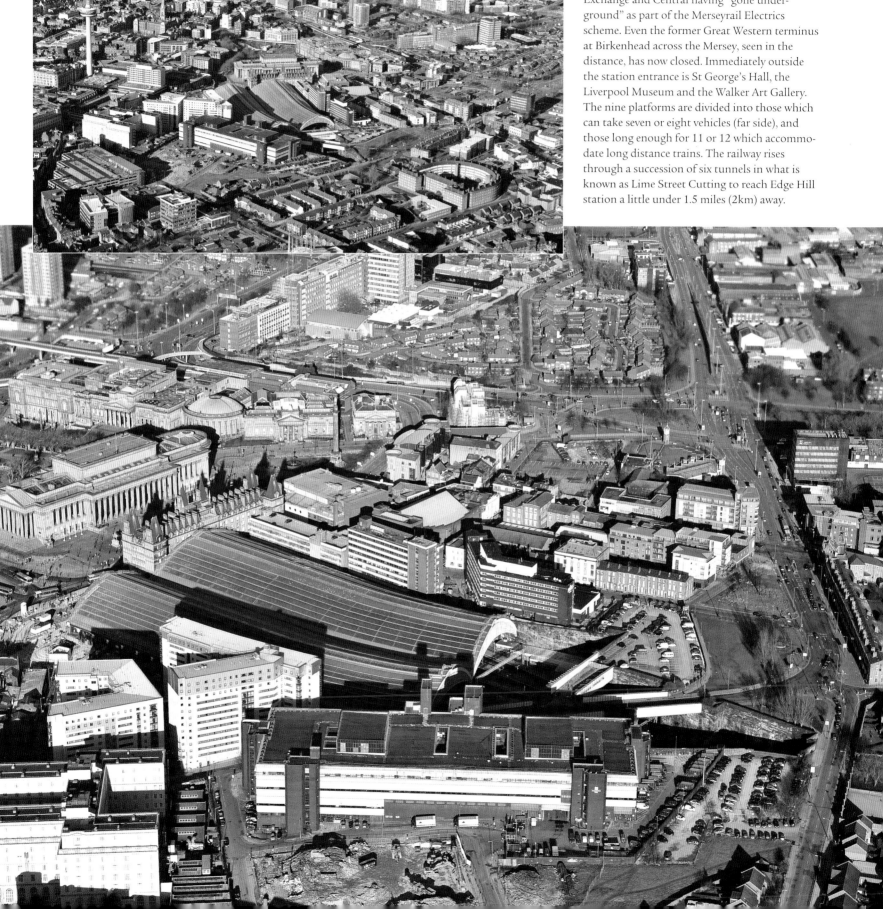

Liverpool

Today, Lime Street station is the only above ground station in central Liverpool, with both Exchange and Central having "gone underground" as part of the Merseyrail Electrics scheme. Even the former Great Western terminus at Birkenhead across the Mersey, seen in the distance, has now closed. Immediately outside the station entrance is St George's Hall, the Liverpool Museum and the Walker Art Gallery. The nine platforms are divided into those which can take seven or eight vehicles (far side), and those long enough for 11 or 12 which accommodate long distance trains. The railway rises through a succession of six tunnels in what is known as Lime Street Cutting to reach Edge Hill station a little under 1.5 miles (2km) away.

Burnley *above*

Burnley was opened in 1849 as a station on the Lancashire & Yorkshire Railway line from Bury and Blackburn to Colne. The station suffered from rail cutbacks in the 1960s and 1980s and is now a single line with one platform in use. It offers services to Colne and Blackpool South via Preston. The photograph shows Burnley Viaduct, with Burnley Central station just off the photograph to the right. The viaduct consists of 15 rock-faced masonry arches straddling the river Calder below.

Lancaster *right*

Lancaster station, opened in 1846, was designed by railway architect Sir William Tite who also built local stations at Carlisle and Carnforth. In 1902 the station was re-modelled in a mock-Elizabethan style to mirror the original station and nearby Lancaster Castle. At the southern end there is a square tower surmounted by a turret roofed in pyramid style. The northern end is more domestic in form. The station was once known as Lancaster Castle to distinguish it from the former Lancaster Green Ayre station and the castle can be seen in the view looking east. The crossing of the river Lune is out of sight, to the left. Local services run from here to Morecambe and then over the Pennines to Leeds, and also via the coast road and Barrow-in-Furness to Carlisle.

Arnside *above*

The dramatic estuary of the river Kent is crossed by the Furness Railway's Kent Viaduct to the west of Arnside, seen here with the village of Storth beyond. By train it takes around five minutes to travel the 3.27 miles (5.27km) from Arnside to Grange-over-Sands. To make the same journey by road one has to follow the side of the estuary north to Levens Bridge and cross the river there – a distance of around 16 miles (26km). Further west, the estuary of the river Leven is also crossed by a rail bridge, cutting a huge amount of time and distance off the journey by road.

Carlisle *below*

This photograph looks east to the border railway station of Carlisle with the castle beyond. For many years this attractive station was known as Carlisle Citadel. It was built in 1847 and expanded in 1875-6 with the arrival of the Midland Railway. The imposing façade was designed in 1847 by Sir William Tite, architect of the Bank of England and the Royal Exchange in London. Carlisle station is a major junction; at one time it was the converging point of the Maryport & Carlisle, the London & North Western, the Midland, the North British and Caledonian Railways.

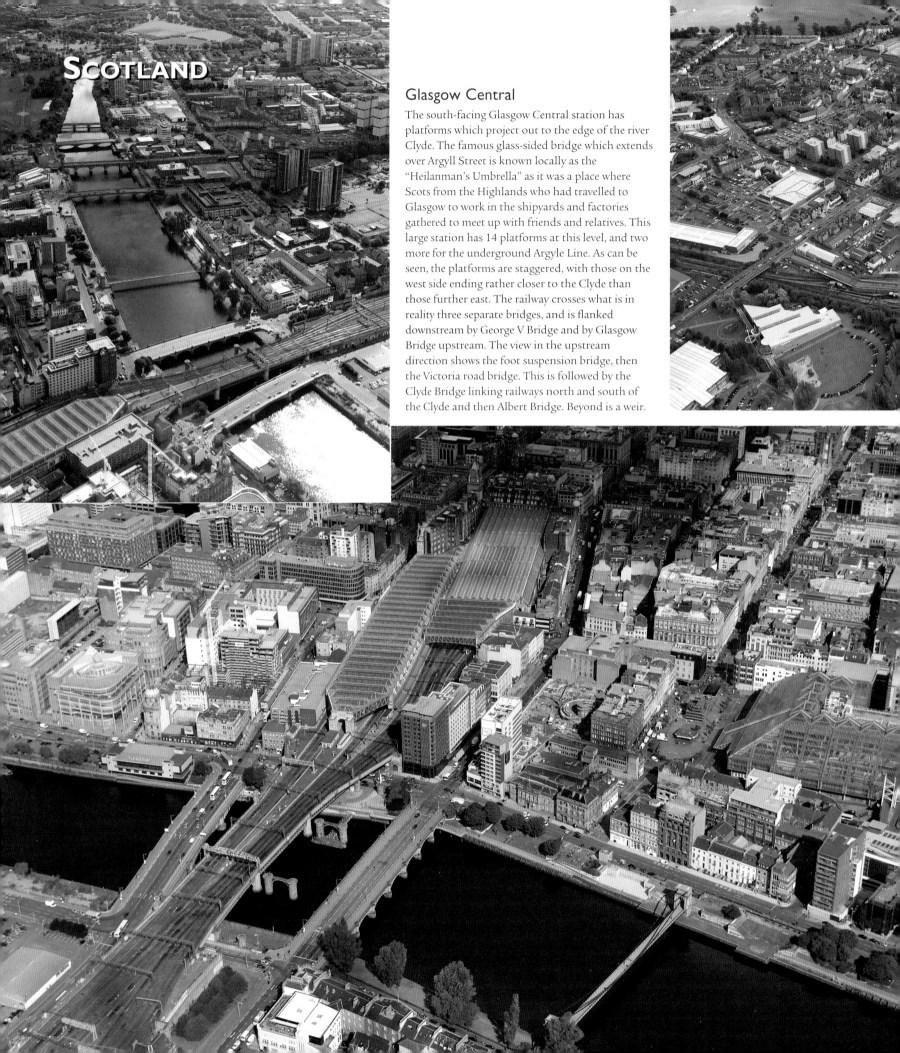

SCOTLAND

Glasgow Central

The south-facing Glasgow Central station has platforms which project out to the edge of the river Clyde. The famous glass-sided bridge which extends over Argyll Street is known locally as the "Heilanman's Umbrella" as it was a place where Scots from the Highlands who had travelled to Glasgow to work in the shipyards and factories gathered to meet up with friends and relatives. This large station has 14 platforms at this level, and two more for the underground Argyle Line. As can be seen, the platforms are staggered, with those on the west side ending rather closer to the Clyde than those further east. The railway crosses what is in reality three separate bridges, and is flanked downstream by George V Bridge and by Glasgow Bridge upstream. The view in the upstream direction shows the foot suspension bridge, then the Victoria road bridge. This is followed by the Clyde Bridge linking railways north and south of the Clyde and then Albert Bridge. Beyond is a weir.

Perth *left*

This is an interesting example of how the coming together of two railway lines, from Inverness left, and from Dundee top, confined the main development of the city to the area in between. Even then, the Caledonian Railway station is spread over a substantial area, and room also had to be found for the carriage shed. The line to the right continues to Stirling or Ladybank. The river Tay is seen in the distance, crossed by a bridge carrying the railway to Dundee.

Inverness *below*

When the Highland Railway reached Inverness from Perth and from Aberdeen, the position of the terminus was quite reasonably placed as near to the town centre as it could get. However, the lines to the far north and to Kyle of Lochalsh in the west needed to cross the river Ness (seen in the distance). This required a very tight curve from the terminus (similar to that constructed at Brighton station) to make the connection. Again there is an avoiding line, but its use is effectively confined to freight. A traction depot is situated in the triangle of lines created and beyond this there are extensive facilities for passenger stock maintenance, for storage and for freight.

London St Pancras International

In 1868, when contemplating their new London terminus at St Pancras, the Midland Railway's intention was to produce a set of buildings that would impress the capital. The site itself was not promising as the Grand Union Canal to the north restricted entry to trains heading in and out of the station. Years earlier, in 1852, on the neighbouring site at King's Cross, the Great Northern had taken the decision to route their lines under the canal. But the Midland Railway's aim was to outdo every other station in London and with St Pancras they certainly achieved their ambition. It is difficult to over-rate the station. The roof designed by the Midland's consulting engineer William Henry Barlow was the widest in the world at the time and the range of bricks, brick bondings and stone dressings used in the construction of the train shed is remarkable. Sir George

Gilbert Scott's High Victorian Gothic design for the station buildings and the hotel was ornate but stopped short of vulgarity. Every aspect of the station's layout was carefully planned. Even the columns supporting the building below platform level were designed to store the beer barrels which the company itself transported from its Burton-on-Trent brewery. The station went from strength to strength until the early years of the 20th century when traffic began to decline. By the 1980s, St Pancras did not have enough passengers to earn its keep and its future seemed bleak. But the decision in 1996 to route Eurostar services through east London led to a change in its fortunes. The eventual result was a substantial reconstruction and renovation, and the station has become the home of the Eurostar service as well as East Midlands trains and the high-speed services of

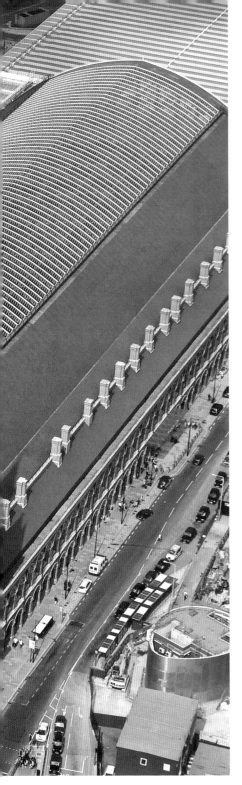

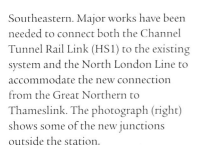

Southeastern. Major works have been needed to connect both the Channel Tunnel Rail Link (HS1) to the existing system and the North London Line to accommodate the new connection from the Great Northern to Thameslink. The photograph (right) shows some of the new junctions outside the station.

Cricklewood *above*

In his poem *Parliament Hill Fields,* written towards the end of the Second World War, Sir John Betjeman describes a train "Rumbling under blackened girders, Midland, bound for Cricklewood." The scene today would not be recognised by the poet. The station has three island platforms but not a smut in sight. This view is looking north; the line proceeding to the left is the Dudding Hill Curve, which takes freight trains to Acton.

Bedford *right*

This view looks east over Bedford on the Midland Main Line. The nearest two tracks (one without a platform) are for the use of long-distance East Midlands sevices to and from Sheffield or Nottingham. The remainder are electrified, though the East Midlands Line uses the loop in the up direction and it is an East Midland train that is seen in this photograph. Thameslink services run from here through the capital and then as far south as Brighton; both towns are around 50 miles (80km) from central London. Journey times are about 2hrs 15mins, with four trains an hour. There is also a stopping service to Bletchley.

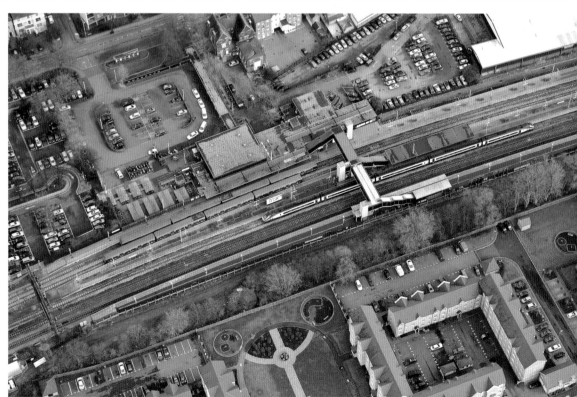

Luton *above*

This substantial town has three stations: the main station at Luton (previously named Luton Midland Road) seen here, Leagrave 2.5 miles (4km) to the north-west of Luton and Luton Airport Parkway on the south-eastern periphery of the town close to the ring road, built to serve Luton Airport. The photograph is looking towards London with the slow lines on the left. The station has five platforms, which include reversing facilities and carriage sidings. Beyond, the line curves to the right and Luton Airport can be seen in the distance.

Luton Airport Parkway *left*

This station was constructed in 1999 to serve passengers at Luton Aiport. The station is served by trains from the East Midlands and from the capital. Sadly, the station lies some distance west of the airport and requires a bus transfer. The utilitarian station is seen in this view looking north-west with a Thameslink train calling at the station.

Nottingham *above*

The fine red brick frontage of Nottingham station was designed by local architect Albert Edward Lambert as part of its reconstruction by the Midland Railway in 1900. The station entrance is situated on a bridge, straddling the railway. It leads to the booking hall with steps down to two large covered island platforms. To the right, where the train is standing, is platform six, which is used mainly for football traffic. To the left of the footbridge, halfway along the platforms, the terminus of the Nottingham Express Transit light rail system can be seen. The watercourse is the Nottingham & Beeston Canal.

Sheffield *left*

For practical purposes, Sheffield is the northern extremity of East Midlands services from London. For Leeds, it is quicker to travel from King's Cross. This large station is the centre of a number of local and regional services, and also the Cross Country route from the North East to the South West. In 2006 the station and Sheaf Square, the public space to the front, were refurbished and are now known as "the Gateway to Sheffield". Looking from the south, the station would appear to have more than eight platforms. And so it has – if suffixes like "1a" and "1b" are counted separately there are a total of 16. To the right can be seen Sheffield Supertram, with a tram in view. The tram line crosses the railway and then turns left to the city centre, using the bridge to the north of the station.

Ribblehead *left*

The Midland's bold creation of its own independent route from Settle to Carlisle to capture traffic to and from Scotland required some magnificent engineering. The route contains a number of viaducts, of which Ribblehead has to be the most impressive. It is 1,320ft (406m) long, 104ft (32m) high and has 24 arches, each with a span of 45ft (14m). This view is from the eastern side of the line, and the extent of the Ribblehead settlement, centring on The Railway Inn, is plain to see. Remarkably there is a station (off picture to the left), offering a good commuter service to Leeds. The train starts from here at 07.14, arriving in Leeds at 08.36. Return evening trains leave Leeds at 17.56 and 19.19. Not bad for a rural journey of 52 miles each way!

Settle *right*

This pleasant town has a neat and well-kept station and is the real beginning of the "long drag", as it was known in the days of steam, with an unremitting 1 in 100 gradient until reaching the summit at Kirkby Stephen, 30 miles (48km) away. A service for Carlisle is waiting in the station.

EAST COAST MAIN LINE

The East Coast main line from London King's Cross to Edinburgh and Aberdeen, with a secondary route to Leeds, is a fast track for trains in a way that the West Coast never was and never could be. Superbly engineered, it has long stretches of straight track or very nearly so. The few serious curves such as the one at Peterborough have largely been eliminated although those at York and Newcastle still impose severe speed restrictions. The north-east was the cradle of railways and at its heart was railway pioneer George Stephenson, "the father of railways" who was born at Wylam, Northumberland, in 1781. Stephenson built the first railway in the world to use steam, the Stockton to Darlington line in 1825, and he rose from pit boy to become the President of the Institution of Mechanical Engineers. Followed by other rail pioneers such as his son Robert and Isambard Kingdom Brunel, Stephenson founded a system of engineering and transport which would spread all over the world.

London King's Cross

The southern terminus of the East Coast Main Line was opened in 1852 by the Great Northern Railway. King's Cross station consists of two large train sheds with a suburban station alongside. The train sheds held eight platforms, numbered 1-8; in 2010 a platform 0 was added to the east side (on the left in the photograph). Beyond the three platforms of the suburban station stands the Great Northern Hotel. In the foreground, the tracks disappear into Gasworks Tunnel to pass under the Grand Union Canal; this has always been a constraint on the maximum train lengths that could

be accommodated in the station. To the right is Goods Way leading round to the new ticket office area of St Pancras. The roof of the station was extended to accommodate the Eurostars; as can be seen, the new roof is a little longer than the old. Both King's Cross and St Pancras face on to Euston Road. However, new construction still under way in the photograph will effectively move the focus of both stations into the central area. York Way runs up the side of King's Cross; at the junction with Goods Way is the headquarters of Network Rail.

Finsbury Park *above*

This view of the busy Finsbury Park station is from the east. The station entrance is in the narrow neck between Seven Sisters Road (left) and Stroud Green Road (right). Apart from being a National Rail station, Finsbury Park is an interchange with the Victoria and Piccadilly Lines of London Underground which share the same station premises.

Bounds Green *below*

This traction maintenance depot is situated beyond Alexandra Palace station on the beginning of the Hertford branch. It handles all repairs and maintenance for East Coast Main Line trains. The depot stands close to the now demolished Palace Gates station built to serve nearby Alexandra Palace.

Hornsey *above*

This photograph shows the busy four-track East Coast Line from just north of Harringay platforms through to Alexandra Palace, a distance of about 1.5 miles (2.5km). The flyover in the foreground was built to keep the freight using Ferme Park yard on the left clear of other traffic. Hornsey traction depot is on the right; this is "home" for all the electric units used on the King's Cross-based services to Peterborough and King's Lynn as well as Welwyn Garden City and Hertford North.

Peterborough *below*

This is the first major stop on the East Coast Main Line and the end of suburban services out of London. Peterborough is a connecting point into the railways of East Anglia and offers a link towards Nuneaton and Birmingham. This view looks south and the line to Ely is seen here crossing the river Nene and then passing under the East Coast Line. The station was the subject of a major reconstruction in the 1970s, which removed a 20mph (32kph) speed limit and added platforms to make today's total of five.

Doncaster *left*

The Railway Works at Doncaster were established by the Great Northern Railway in 1853 and can be seen here in the foreground of this photograph. Beyond them is the station with its eight platforms and with fast lines up and down through the middle. The river Don is also featured, meandering slowly eastwards. At the north end of the station a complex of roads crosses over the track, which are always noticeable when passing underneath in a train.

Leeds *above*

Leeds City station is the busiest in the north of England and the
third busiest in the UK outside London after Birmingham New
Steet and Glasgow Central. The current station is a 1960s rebuild
which saw the old Leeds Central station disappear. Now called
Leeds, it has since been further rebuilt to cope with growing
traffic. This view looking east sees the short platforms for local
services to Skipton, Ilkley and Harrogate on the left, the station
entrance (out of sight), then the main line platforms and those
for local services to a host of destinations. Most trains leave from
this, the west end. At the eastern end the railway narrows to two
tracks for a while, with only three routes available beyond Neville
Hill depot. Beside and underneath the station is the river Aire and
in the foreground is the connection to the Leeds & Liverpool
Canal. From the station, the area to the left is the business
district, ahead is the main shopping area, and to the right enter-
tainment and the markets. The road under the station is not
pleasant to use, and there is public pressure to provide a second
station entrance on the south side.

Knaresborough *above*

Rail engineers faced a considerable challenge in the town of Knaresborough because of the town's location on a gorge of the river Nidd. In this delightful view, the approach from Harrogate (left) is level. The train then crosses the high viaduct over the river Nidd, goes over the level crossing and enters the station. There is then a short 534ft (164m) tunnel at the far end of the platforms. The whole photograph shows the skills needed by Victorian engineers in getting their levels right. The train then continues to York. The line was opened in 1848, and the stretch between Leeds and York via Harrogate is full of interest for the traveller.

Pannal *left*

The massive and impressive 31-arch Crimple viaduct is 1,710ft (525m) long and lies south-east of Pannal station. Situated on the outskirts of Harrogate, the viaduct is on the line to Leeds. This beautiful structure provides fine views across the valley as it crosses Crimple Beck.

York

This majestic station, situated close to the walls of the ancient city, is one of Britain's most important railway junctions and is roughly midway between London and Edinburgh. It is home to the National Railway Museum which can be seen in the foreground of the photograph with the station behind and the city in the distance; York Minster is top left. The photograph emphasises the curve in the track, one of the few examples on the East Coast Main Line. The branch line to Scarborough is shown leaving on its bridge over the river Ouse; trains for Newcastle continue north. The large building on the right of the station is the Station Hotel. The station has 11 platforms connected by a wide footbridge, extended to provide a direct route to the museum. From top to bottom, the following museum exhibits are visible in the photograph (right):

· the Museum's own Class 03 shunter, a Mk1 gangwayed brake and a Metro-Cammell Pullman The Triangle Bar;
· an English Electric Class 40, a War Department Austerity 2-10-0, and Bulleid 0-6-0 freight tender locomotive no C1;
· a specially produced "container" to house a Freightliner guard, an English Electric Class 20 and Britannia 4-6-2 no 70013 *Oliver Cromwell*;
· the prototype Advanced Passenger Train (APT);
· Beattie 2-4-0WT no 30587 and a USA 0-6-0T in Southern malachite green.

Scarborough

Scarborough remains a popular seaside destination and this view of the station looks towards the sea; the station was built with a clocktower designed to summon day-trippers on the long trudge up from the beach. Filey and Bridlington are also popular resorts but Scarborough can be reached from many towns in Yorkshire without a change of train. Most of the station's platforms are designed for all year-round traffic and can accommodate trains with seven to nine carriages but there is one extremely long excursion platform which can cater for 13 carriages. This platform and the one next to it are double-sided for at least part of their lengths. This allowed passengers to join or alight from either side of the train.

Darlington *above*

This is an important station serving Teesside as well as the local area. The station has a capacious roof; despite its size there are only four platforms below. This 2008 view was taken looking south towards London; as can be seen the main lines for non-stopping trains by-pass the station on the left. There was once a train announcer at King's Cross who always articulated the station name as "Darling-ton", with feeling. It endeared her to many of the male staff working within earshot!

Brotton *right*

Railways along the thinly populated Cleveland and North Yorkshire coast mostly suffered an early demise, with the closure of passenger lines taking place from the 1950s onwards. There were however a few exceptions, such as the line beyond Saltburn West Junction to the potash mines at Boulby. This was, and still is, retained for freight. The route takes a huge u-shaped detour to circumnavigate Warsett Hill which, at 550ft (169m), is seen here rising to the right. In this splendid photograph a Freightliner locomotive hauls 13 vehicles towards the mine on 30 June 2008. At this point there is about six miles to go. Debris on the beach from a cliff-fall shows the problems of operating in such conditions but the long-distance Cleveland Way footpath still manages to squeeze itself between the railway fence and the cliff edge. By no stretch of the imagination could this be described as a high-speed railway but the line is very picturesque.

Sunderland

The twin road and rail bridges seen in the photograph cross the river Wear to the north of Sunderland city centre. Uniquely, the Queen Alexandra railway bridge carries both main line trains and Tyne and Wear Metro services on the same tracks. To the right, trains enter a tunnel and they remain below ground while in the city centre. Sunderland station itself lies under the central shopping area and serves both main line and Metro services. On the left can just be seen the ends of the platforms of St Peter's, a station served by Metro trains only.

Newcastle

Designed by architect John Dobson in the neo-Classical style, the beautiful Newcastle station was opened by Queen Victoria in 1850. It has 12 platforms and is built on a curve; all the lines are electrified. Below left are Newcastle's famous bridges. Starting from the front they are the Tyne Road Bridge, the swing bridge, the High Level rail and road bridge (rail above road), the Queen Elizabeth II Metro bridge, the King Edward rail bridge, and the Redheugh road bridge.

The railway in Newcastle is flexible; trains leaving from Newcastle station to London can start in either direction, travel either via the King Edward bridge (normal route) or the High Level bridge (if the train needs to be turned around) and continue on the main line south. Passengers may find this a bit unnerving if the train starts in the "wrong" direction and they are not warned of what is about to happen. Below right, this photograph shows the Castle Keep in the junction of lines at the far end of the station. Here, the line to Edinburgh leaves to the left. Visitors to the keep can enjoy a panoramic view of the city as well as the railway. The photograph above shows a Virgin Cross-County train leaving Newcastle on the King Edward Bridge, passing an incoming GNER train. These photographs were taken on 25 September 2007. Since then the franchises have changed hands and the liveries are now different.

Edinburgh *above*

The Scottish capital's main station is known to many as Waverley, to distinguish it from nearby Haymarket, although officially the station is just called Edinburgh. This view looks towards Haymarket and Princes Street Gardens and shows the wide expanse of the station roof, with North Bridge from its junction with Princes Street crossing over the station's eastern section. The station is the second-largest in terms of area in the UK after London Waterloo. It stands in the narrow valley which traverses Edinburgh from east to west between the medieval old town and the Georgian New Town. All of the station and its 20 platforms are now electrified.

Forth Bridge *right*

The Forth Rail Bridge dates from 1890 and was designed by Sir John Fowler and Sir Benjamin Baker; it is 1.5 miles (2.5km) long and is a steel bridge of cantilever construction. Maintenance is a major expense and the slightly bandaged look of the bridge reflects the constant work required to keep the structure in good condition. Just upstream is the Forth Road Bridge which dates from 1964 when it replaced the centuries-old ferry services across the Forth. The usefulness of both bridges cannot be questioned; the next crossing point on the Firth of Forth by road is at Kincardine, fully 15 miles (24km) away and rail passengers would need to travel inland via Stirling. The esteem in which the Forth Bridge is held can be judged by its appearance on the 2004 pound coin; it also features on Scottish banknotes.

Dundee

Dundee station is in a cutting and
immediately after leaving the
platforms the line dives into a tunnel
en route for Aberdeen. The tunnel is
below sea level. The station consists
of a large island, with two south-facing
bays. With some sidings on the right,
the line then splits with one branch
heading straight on to Perth and the
other south over the Tay Bridge to
Leuchars and then on to Edinburgh.
Including the approaches, the Tay
Bridge is 2.25 miles (3.6km) long.
The present structure dates from 1887
and replaced that lost in a very severe
winter gale, known as the Tay Bridge
Disaster, in 1879. On that night a
train, together with a substantial
portion of the bridge, was blown
into the river Tay after dark. There
were no survivors.

ANGLIA

Because of the geography of East Anglia, its railways are physically largely separated from the rest of the system, although there is considerable freight traffic to and from the expanding East Coast ports such as Felixstowe which links up with the Midlands and North. Many of the earliest railways in eastern England catered for the small agricultural towns scattered across the area, transporting produce to markets in Norwich, Ipswich or London. Other lines developed to link East Anglian towns and cities with the capital; the line from London to Cambridge, for example, developed to link London with the ancient university city. In the mid-19th century the development of East Anglian seaside towns would not have been possible without the railways. Cromer, for example, was a favourite of wealthy families from Norwich who used the railways to travel from the city to their summer homes on the coast. Now East Anglia's railways, particularly in the south of the region, largely cater for commuters heading south to the capital for work.

London Liverpool Street

The original London Liverpool Street was built in two halves, the west side in 1874-5 and the east side in 1894. The approach to the station was gloomy and it was usually smoke-wreathed in the days of steam trains. The station never really formed a coherent whole and its total reconstruction in 1991 as one station by British Rail was a major triumph. The Great Eastern Hotel (the brown brick building at the front of the station on Liverpool Street itself) remains much as it was originally built, with station entrances on the left-hand side and also from Bishopsgate on the right. Behind are the train sheds and you can just see how the railway curves to the right on leaving the station and then passes under Bishopsgate shortly before reaching the crossroads with Great Eastern Street and Commercial Street. At this point Bishopsgate becomes Shoreditch High Street and further north this is crossed by a bowstring girder bridge. The bridge carries the East London Line which opened in 2010. The sweep of the new line can be traced from Hoxton (top centre) and on the viaduct round to Shoreditch High Street station. This above ground station has been deliberately constructed with space below and on either side so that a future commercial development can be accommodated.

Hackney Downs *above*

The station platforms at Hackney Downs on the Great Eastern are just to the north of where the railway is crossed by the North London Line. The nearest station on the North London Line is Hackney Central to the east, far enough away to make an awkward interchange between the two stations. The Graham Road curve on the right was used for a time to enable North London trains originating from Watford Junction to reach Liverpool Street. This followed the closure of the City terminus of Broad Street in 1986.

Hertford East *right*

This view of Hertford East on the Great Eastern Main Line looks east, from the ornate station buildings at this terminus, down the platforms towards Broxbourne. The former route to Hertford North (Great Northern) is still just about visible to the left, although there is a considerable amount of derelict land in between. This was part of the 1960 "Chenford" electrification, the acronym standing for Chingford, Enfield and Bishop's Stortford.

King's Lynn *left*

The railway arrived in King's Lynn in 1846; the current building dates from 1871 and is a typical Great Eastern Railway design, with two platforms in general use plus carriage sidings. A short branch line to the docks was opened in 1862 and there is still a three-mile (5km) section to Middleton Towers to a sand quarry at Dereham. The locomotive on the branch line is able to turn around by continuing on a loop line close to King's Lynn docks.

Ely *below*

Ely station was modernised in the 1990s when the line was electrified. It has one side platform and one island, where several trains reverse. This includes services such as those between Birmingham and Norwich; the only alternative to reversing at Ely is to omit the station altogether. The level crossing beyond the platform ends is used mostly by heavy goods and similar vehicles; for other traffic there is an underpass. Much of the road and rail layout of the town is dictated by the waterways, the river Great Ouse in particular, and the means by which it was bridged. This photograph shows the famous Ely Cathedral (top left) nicknamed "the ship of the Fens" overlooking the city

Stratford

This view shows the Great Eastern main line on a north west diagonal through the site, with the Central Line of London Underground to the right. Further right is the building which gives access to the terminus of the Docklands Light Railway from Poplar, the Jubilee Line of London Underground and the DLR line from Canning Town to Stratford International, then under construction.

Beyond is the bus station. Bottom centre is the connection to the North London Line used by London Overground and freight. The wide brown bridge across the whole gives pedestrian access from the main Stratford station to the Westfield Stratford shopping centre and thence to the Olympic Park, the centrepiece of the 2012 Olympic Games.

Stratford International

Stratford International station is contained in a box with the platforms at low level. International platforms need to be separated from those used for domestic purposes, for customs and immigration reasons. The single line running through the centre of the station and rising to the surface is designed to take empty trains to and from the Eurostar depot at Temple Mills. The passenger terminal facilities are seen above the box in an embryonic state of construction. The general scene in 2010 shows the same station box, but this time from the High Meads end. The junction in the foreground is Stratford International West Junction, which will take trains (left) to the North London Line or (right) to Stratford itself. The other direction leads to Temple Mills East Junction. In the distance is the curve of the Central Line on its way to Leyton but now without any connection to the national rail network. To the left of this is the bridge carrying the A12 road. On the far side of this is the reception area for the Eurostar depot.

Gidea Park

This station is a normal suburban two island platform construction. The station was first opened in 1910, as Squirrel's Heath and Gidea Park. The station was provided with sidings so that the electric trains working the line to Shenfield (which was electrified in 1949) could be parked overnight. The sidings were also a convenient point to terminate inner suburban services. The sidings are beyond the station on the down side and there are five in total. A centre siding between the two working lines was also built. This made it possible to reverse a train back to Liverpool Street without blocking any other line in the process. To the far left are the two fast lines.

Witham *above*

The modest station at Witham on the line from Liverpool Street to Norwich is the junction for the Braintree branch, which can just be seen at the top left. Braintree is mostly served by through trains from London but the availability of a separate platform allows for a shuttle service if required. It also gives the ability to hold a train if necessary for connections in the opposite direction. There are passing loops in both directions at Witham. That on the up side of the station was used for many years by the branch service from Maldon but that was withdrawn in 1964. These loops are the only ones in which freight can be taken off the main lines in the 47 miles (75km) between Stratford and Colchester.

Colchester *above & left*

Colchester boasts a massive up platform, so long that even this aerial photograph does not include it all. Careful inspection will reveal that the up platform is split into two separate parts forming platforms three and four. The split means that each platform is in reality on a separate line. Between them the two platforms can accommodate 27 vehicles. South of the station can be seen the small locomotive facility and the carriage sidings where trains are being moved into position. Beyond both of these are the engineer's sidings and beyond that part of the car park. Colchester station is well to the north of the town centre and the fast railway services offered from here attract commuters from a wide area.

Ipswich *below & right*

This view of Ipswich shows the passenger station and the tunnel approach from the south. The locomotive fuelling point and carriage sidings are on the right. The station has a side platform for up trains plus a north-facing bay; on the down side there is a single island. Local services from here run to Felixstowe, Lowestoft, and via Bury St Edmunds to Cambridge or Peterborough; main line services from London run to Norwich. Behind the point where the photograph has been taken there are substantial freight yards serving the port of Felixstowe and Ipswich. From here freight trains proceed to Nuneaton and the West Midlands, the north-west or London. The route to Ipswich Docks is owned by Associated British Ports. The road to the left leads to the town centre, across the river Orwell. The route of the docks railway, no longer in regular use, can be traced alongside the Orwell (below).

Upminster *below*

Upminster station is the base for three separate rail services. The first is the main line Tilbury service, which uses platforms two and three on the far side and also the bay, platform one, for local routes. The second user is London Underground, who provide stopping services to central London and links to the Underground network. The Underground uses platforms 4, 5 and 6 for District Line services, which terminate here and one of the trains is visible in the photograph. The third service, on platform 7, is the Romford-Upminster shuttle. These three operations are entirely separate and the physical connections between them in a railway sense do not exist, except that they operate here from the same location. Upminster underground is the eastern terminus of the District Line and the most easterly station on the London Underground network.

London Fenchurch Street

This pocket-sized city terminus runs trains to Southend via Basildon or Tilbury. Some consider Fenchurch Street station to be tucked away off the beaten track but this aerial view with the station diagonally across the picture shows that it is close to Tower Bridge and the Tower of London. Centre left is Tower Gateway station on the Docklands Light Railway. Fenchurch Street was opened in 1841 and is one of the smallest terminals in London with only four platforms. The photograph shows the DLR station and the very limited space occupied by Fenchurch Street itself. Despite this, Fenchurch Street handles 20 incoming trains in the busiest peak hour. The entire operation uses 74 4-carriage trains, which run in formations of up to 12 carriages. The whole operation has to be organised with military precision during rush hours so that trains don't deliver passengers faster than they can safely clear the platforms, stairways, escalators and exits.

TRANSPORT FOR LONDON

Transport for London (TfL) runs the Docklands Light Railway, London Underground and London Overground. The Docklands Light Railway (DLR) is an expanding light rail system whose lines radiate from Poplar. Initially the system was set up to serve the redeveloped docklands area but it has now expanded further east and into south-east London. The DLR runs mostly above ground level with some underground sections including two crossings of the Thames at Greenwich and Woolwich. The system operates by drawing electricity from a third rail along the track; this third rail is "covered" to protect it from snow and ice. London Underground is the oldest underground system in the world serving 270 stations above and below ground mainly north of the Thames. London Overground covers an orbital route round the capital using five existing and revamped Network Rail lines. The system includes the pioneering Thames Tunnel which carries the East London Line between Rotherhithe and Wapping. This was the first railway tunnel to be built under a river anywhere in the world; the engineers were Mark Brunel and his son Isambard.

Poplar *left*

Poplar is at the heart of the Docklands Light Railway system serving three out of the four routes on the system. The original 1987 depot for 11 cars can be seen in the centre of the photograph. The system has been extended several times. Poplar was a station on the

DOCKLANDS LIGHT RAILWAY

initial DLR system which opened in 1987, but was later extensively re-built and enlarged. In 1999 the DLR expanded south across the Thames to Lewisham and in 2009 a further extension was built to Woolwich Arsenal. The DLR fleet now consists of 149 cars; trains have also been increased in length from a single artic-ulated car to three. The DLR network is now 19 miles (31km) long and has 40 stations. The view above looks west to Poplar station where the routes diverge: left and across the dock to Canary Wharf or straight on to Bank or Tower Gateway.

Bow Creek

The lazy river winding down to the Thames is Bow Creek. Through this the Docklands Light Railway picks a curvaceous route taking it to Canning Town in the distance. From here the DLR can continue to Beckton or Woolwich Arsenal. At Canning Town passengers can change to reach Stratford International or transfer to the Jubilee Line. The major road is the A13 East India Dock Road, with the A124 Barking Road diverging from it; in the foreground is the A1020 Lower Lea Crossing, with the East India Dock Basin and then the Thames below.

119

London Underground

Upminster depot *above*

This major London Underground depot opened in 1958. It occupies a large site to the east of Upminster station and carries out cleaning and maintenance work on District Line trains. The depot's position beyond the end of the station platforms means that it is convenient to remove trains from service and then to slot them back into position afterwards. The photograph shows the normal six-car set-up of District Line trains with one half-set of three cars being shunted. Note how the walking routes across the tracks are prominently marked in yellow paint and how all trains are parked clear of them.

Hammersmith *right*

The photograph (right) shows Hammersmith station, the western terminus of the Hammersmith & City Line and Circle Line. A short distance away is the entirely separate Hammersmith station which serves the District and Piccadilly Lines. Hammersmith station was once on a branch jointly promoted by the Metropolitan and the London and South Western Railway. It has long been part of the Underground and in 2009 the Circle Line began to operate from the station. The platform canopies cover the whole length of the platforms, rather than about half as is commonplace on many LU stations.

Earl's Court *left*

This shows the eastern end of the District Line at Earl's Court station; the Piccadilly Line is in the tunnel below. The station here has a light and airy glazed roof, which helps to brighten the often crowded platforms. This is the junction for trains to Edgware Road and central London (beyond) and in the other direction to Wimbledon, Richmond, Ealing Broadway and Kensington Olympia. This means that the station is a busy interchange, and also serves the Earl's Court Exhibition Centre. The photograph shows how the station is squeezed tightly into the middle of a residential area.

East Putney *below*

In this view from the south, the two routes are the District Line towards the Thames and Putney Bridge and a route used mainly for empty South West Trains between Waterloo and Wimbledon depot. The main line which this joins can just be seen in a cutting, crossing the photograph. The whole is one of those historical accidents of railway geography, mainly to do with competition for territory between companies, and later coming to terms to get the best use out of the result. As to who owned, or presently owns what, that is a story in itself.

Loughton *right*

Opened in 1940 but not used by the Underground until 1948, Loughton station was part of an expansion of the Central Line along a main line run by the Eastern Counties railway. The station is of notable architectural significance. It was designed by the architect John Murray Easton, whose work includes the Royal Horticultural Hall in London. The gull-winged canopies on the station platform and the lofty arched ticket hall are particularly striking. The extra centre platform was built to allow the option for trains to terminate here and to arrive and leave in both directions.

Hainault depot *below*

The Central Line has two depots at West Ruislip, and the one seen here, at Hainault. This is the loop from Leytonstone to Woodford via Newbury Park. This photograph shows the northern end, where over 20 parallel tracks converge to a shunting neck. The line from Hainault to Woodford can just be seen at the bottom of the photograph.

Stanmore above

Built by the Metropolitan in 1932, Stanmore station was transferred to the Bakerloo in 1939 and again to the Jubilee Line in 1979. Stanmore is the northernmost station on the Jubilee Line. It was constructed with a modest island platform, designed so that the line could be extended at a later date. In 2009 a third platform was added, which gives more flexibility to the line and allows more opportunities for service recovery when things go wrong.

Stratford Market left

This eye-catching depot was built for the Jubilee Line extension, which opened in 1999. The award-winning building contains offices and the workshop, where under train cleaning, repairs, general inspection and body lifting off the running gear take place. Outside there are around 20 storage sidings and the fronts of trains can be seen projecting from many of them. To the right are the tracks from West Ham to the Stratford terminus which lies beyond the top of the picture.

Neasden depot *above*

Neasden was the nerve centre of the Metropolitan Railway, with extensive overhaul facilities as well as the normal running sheds. The depot also housed the Metropolitan's own power station, now long gone, a feature of early electric railways built when supplies from the National Grid were either non-existent or unreliable. This view shows the sheer size of the depot area, which looks after Metropolitan trains (nearer the camera) and Jubilee Line trains (further away). A Jubilee train can be seen on the line and, bottom left, a Chiltern service is leaving the High Wycombe route.

Wembley Park *left*

This station is an important interchange where passengers transfer between Metropolitan Line services which run non-stop to Finchley Road and the Jubilee which also calls at the intermediate stations. Wembley Park is the principal station used by those attending events at Wembley Stadium and the extensive provision for coping with crowds and dealing with them safely can be seen to the left and behind the main station entrance (bottom, centre). Wembley Park has to cope with daily commuter peaks but on match days the whole nature and scale of train operations changes.

Highgate depot *below*

Seen here behind the Great North Road in the foreground is Highgate depot, a minor and now modernised depot on the Northern Line. In the immediate post-war period, the depot was earmarked for expansion with the expectation that post-war suburban house-building would continue north and north-west to Elstree and Bushey Heath. But electric trains in passenger service were never to pass here. Green Belt planning restrictions limiting the capital's expansion beyond its present limits were introduced from the 1930s and Highgate depot remained a comparative backwater.

Finchley Central *below*

This view shows the former Great Northern Railway station at Finchley Central on the Northern Line, with all three platforms occupied. From the left can be seen trains for Mill Hill East, for High Barnet and for the West End or City branches. The station was originally built in 1867 and still retains much of its original Victorian architecture. In the 1930s, Finchley Central was the home station of Harry Beck, who produced the original schematic diagram of Underground lines.

Pinner *left*

Pinner station opened in 1885 as part of the expansion of the Metropolitan Line into the outer suburbs. It remained as the Metropolitan terminus until 1887 but the company was intent on pressing on with its relentless drive towards the north-west and a link with main lines running to the Midlands and the North. The Metropolitan was eventually extended as far as the hamlet of Verney Junction, just west of Winslow in Buckinghamshire, 50 miles (80km) from Baker Street. But the project eventually ground to a halt and the line closed in 1936. Metropolitan services today terminate at either Watford or Amersham, although Chiltern services continue to Aylesbury Parkway. The photograph shows that Pinner has platforms on the two Watford tracks only.

Arnos Grove

For many years the Great Northern Railway was successful in keeping its rival the Piccadilly Line confined to a northern terminus at Finsbury Park. But in the early 1930s an extension of the Piccadilly Line to Cockfosters was eventually built. It is here at Arnos Grove, reached in 1932, that the line came to the surface and the architect Charles Holden created what many consider his greatest masterpiece in station design. The station is in European-style using concrete, glass and brickwork in geometric shapes – a similar design to those Holden used for other stations on the extension. The drum-shaped ticket hall, seen in both photographs, has a tower announcing itself to the surrounding area, a short walkway leads to the bridge over the covered platforms and there are facilities for buses immediately outside the station entrance.

Northumberland Park depot *above*

The Victoria Line opened in 1968-72. The only place on the line which is above ground is the Northumberland Park depot and the line which approaches it. The depot tracks leave the line at Seven Sisters, and the depot itself is close to Northumberland Park, a National Railway station on the Lea Valley line. The workshops are located in the lower set of sheds in the photograph.

Cockfosters *left*

This is the Piccadilly Line's northern terminus. Like the other stations on the extension from Finsbury Park, Cockfosters was designed by Charles Holden. The station buildings at Cockfosters are low and modest compared to those further down the line at Arnos Grove or Southgate but the tall and elegant glass and concrete canopies over the platforms are striking. The station has three tracks. Trains stopping on the centre track are served by platforms on either side.

LONDON OVERGROUND

New Cross Gate depot *above*

The depot for the East London Line had to be inserted between the main line from London Bridge to New Cross Gate (left) and the East London Line. This night-time photograph looks north across the depot from above New Cross Gate station. To the left of the depot is the new flyover which links the northbound slow line with the East London Line. The main group of maintenance sheds is at the top of the picture and in the brightly lit area are the various depot facilities. To the right can be seen Canal Junction, where the line to New Cross diverges, and beyond that the South Eastern line crossing the East London Line on its way to New Cross.

Dalston Kingsland *right*

The final 1.3 miles (2.1km) northern link of the East London Line from Dalston Junction to Highbury & Islington was a considerable feat of engineering. The tunnel carrying the line had to pass under two road bridges which needed to be strengthened and repaired. Here reconstruction of Boleyn Road bridge is underway. To the right is the link from the North London Line to what is now the East London Line. The line now runs from its northern terminus at Highbury & Islington to New Cross, West Croydon and Crystal Palace south of the Thames.